Disneyland's Hidden Mickeys
Second Edition

DISNEYLAND'S HIDDEN MICKEYS

A Field Guide to

Disneyland Resort®'s

Best Kept Secrets

Second edition

Steven M. Barrett

DISNEYLAND'S HIDDEN MICKEYS

A Field Guide to Disneyland® Resort's
Best Kept Secrets
2nd edition

Published by
The Intrepid Traveler
P.O. Box 531
Branford, CT 06405
http://www.intrepidtraveler.com

Copyright ©2009 by Steven M. Barrett
Second Edition
Printed in Canada
Cover design by Foster & Foster
Interior Design by Starving Artist Design Studio
Maps designed by Evora Taylor
Library of Congress Card Number: 2009922204
ISBN-13: 978-1-887140-85-0

10 9 8 7 6 5 4 3

Trademarks, Etc. • • • • • • • • •

Photo by Vickie Barrett

About the Author. • • • • • • •

Author Steven M. Barrett began hunting Hidden Mickeys at Walt Disney World more than 10 years ago. Convinced that other Disney fans would like to share in the fun of finding these partial or complete images of Mickey Mouse and other Characters that Disney's Imagineers and artists cleverly conceal around the Disney theme parks and other properties, he wrote the book, Hidden Mickeys - A Field Guide to Walt Disney World's Best Kept Secrets. That book, first published in 2003 and now in its fourth edition, offers fans six Hidden Mickey Scavenger Hunts: one for each of the Walt Disney World® Resort's four major theme parks, one for its resort hotels, and one for the rest of WDW—Downtown Disney, the water parks, the golf courses, and so on. Steve organized each Hunt based on his own touring plans (published in his annually updated guidebook, The Hassle-Free Walt Disney World Vacation) so that Hidden Mickey hunters could spend the majority of their time hunting and as little time as possible waiting in lines.

Writing a book wasn't enough for Steve. He next started a website, www.HiddenMickeysGuide.com, so that Hidden Mickey fans could post new and lost sightings from Disney parks around the world. The Disneyland section of his website grew rapidly, so he visited California to organize the Disneyland® Resort Hidden Mickey sightings into a book of their own. The first edition was published in 2007, featuring three Hidden Mickeys Scavenger Hunts, one for Disneyland, one for Disney's California Adventure Park, and one for Downtown Disney, the resort hotels, and other areas on Disneyland property. The second edition you hold in your hand follows that efficient scavenger-hunt format but has been fully updated and expanded to cover many new sightings by Steve and the Hidden Mickey hunters who share their findings on his website.

Steve is a Texas native, Air Force veteran, and former Oklahoma City medical professor. He now lives in the Orlando area, where he practices emergency medicine and makes frequent visits to Walt Disney World.

Dedication . . . .

I dedicate this book to my wife Vickie and our son Steven, who support and help me with my Hidden Mickey passion, and to the many wonderful Hidden Mickey fans I've met through my website and in the Disney parks.

True to their name, Hidden Mickeys are elusive. New ones appear from time to time and some old ones disappear (see page 23, paragraph 2). When that happens — and it will — Steve will let you know on his web site:

www.HiddenMickeysGuide.com

So if you can't find a Mickey — or if you're looking for just a few more — be sure to check it out.

Table of Contents • • • • • • • • •

Maps

Acknowledgements. . . . .

No Hidden Mickey hunter works alone. While I've spotted most of the Hidden Mickeys in this book on my own — and personally verified every single one of them — finding Hidden Mickeys is an ongoing group effort. I am indebted to the following dedicated Hidden Mickey lovers for alerting me to a number of Hidden Mickeys I might otherwise have missed. Thanks to each and every one of you for putting me on the track of one or more of these Disneyland treasures and, in some cases, also helping me verify them.

Names in bold have spotted 10 or more. You can find each person's contribution(s) by visiting my website, www.HiddenMickeysGuide.com. **Extra special thanks to Rosemary and Neil (Finding-Mickey.com)** for spotting and helping me verify over 100 Hidden Mickeys at Disneyland **and to Sharon Dale** for finding over 50.

Karlos Aguilera, Jonathan Agurcia, Kala'i Ahlo-Souza, David Almanza, Antonio Altamirano, Bob Anderson, Katrina Andrews, Cheryl Armstrong, John Axtell, Kristi B., Duane Baker, Hans Balders, Matt and Shelly and Keira Barbieri, Katharine and Ammon Barney, Melisa Beardslee, **Brian Bergstrom**, **Murray Bishop**, Tina Blaylock, Tim Bonanno, Jacob Steven Bonillas, Erik Bratlien, Vicky Braun, Carol Brown, Kaden Brown, Nicolas Brown, Peter Brown, Thierry and Gabriella and Matthieu Bruxelle, Marjorie Burns, Felix Bustos, Peter C., Chris Caflisch, Bev Cain, Stacy Campbell, Marisa Cardenas, Nicholas Noah Carreno, Peter Cefalu, Chelsi Chipps, Diana Cimadamore, Megan Cook, Michelle Cornelius, Marissa Covarrubias, **Josh and Cassi Cox**, **Sharon Dale**, Carlos A. de Alba, Jessica de la Vara, Jeremiah Dempsey, Jacob DePriest, Tim Devine, Matt Dickerson, Casey Dietz, Phillip Donnelly, Tom Donnelly, Maria Dufault, Scott Evans, Joel Feria, Rob Fitzpatrick, Melissa Forte, Keitaro Francisco, Valerie Garren, Michele Galvez, Sam Gennawey, Staci Gleed, Alec Goldberg, Jimmy Golden, Micheline Golden, Reyna Gonzalez, Jordan Goodman, Alex Goslar, Josh Grothem, Kimberly Gryte, Carl H., Dave H., Michael Hadlock, Jon Handler,

Chris Hansen, Cynthia Hess, Kate Heylman, Carl Hoffman, **Milton Holecek**, Michael Hollingsworth, Cory Hughes, Robert Huntington, Molly Jane, **Mike Johansen**, James Johnson, Michelle June, Gordon K., Matt K., Tom K., Summer Kane, **Mehlanie Kayra**, Xela Knarf, Andrew Knight, Matthew and Missy Knoll, Dalia Kuarez, Meghan Kueny-Thornburg, Chase L., Rhonda Lampitt, Phillip Lemon, Andrew Lepire, Annie Lin, Ronald Lindberg, Alysia Lippetti, Myrna Litt, Ryan Lizama, Allison Lloyd, Joe Loecsey, Sal Lugo, Maria Maki, C. Mallonee, Jorge Mario, Dave Marx, **Michael Mason**, Kim McClaughry, Ciara McGovern, Sylvia McNeil, the Miles Family, Randi Miller, Robert Miller, Christopher Morales, Jose Moran, Carlos Moreno, the Muklewicz Family, Andy Neitzert, A. Nelson, Marina Nelson, Ty Nielson, Jen O'Bryan, Michael and Wendy Olayvar, Sam P., Priscilla Padilla, Steve Parmley, Justin Parnell, Cheyenne Pemberton, Jennifer Peterson, Roger Pollard, Diana Poncini, Heather Pone, Melanie Price, Louise Rafferty, Joy E. Robertson-Finley, Jeff Robinson, Jose Rodriguez, Shaun Rosen, Caleb and Richard Ruiz, **Russ Rylee**, John Salinas, Jennifer Salvatierra, Brandie Sargent, Andy Schelb, P. Schwarz, Chris Scott, Kira Scott, Khrys Sganga, Mark Sheppard, the Sherrick family, Zach Simes, Breana Nicole Smith, Brad Steinbrenner, Lloyd Stevens, Darrell St. Pierre, Taylor Stratton, Erin T., Donna Taing, Joseph Thorne, Sandy Thornton, Andrew Thorp, Tim Titus, Christian Urcia, **Luis Valdez**, Ryan Valle, Jeff Van Ry, Kim Vander Dussen, Juliet Violette, Fred Vosecky, Emily W., Mel Waidmann III, Melvin Waidmann II, Rhonda Waidmann, William Waidmann, Barrie and Jack Waldman-Marker, Yvonne Washburn, Christopher Williams, Deb Wills, Laura Wright, Jeanine Yamanaka, and Lynn Yaw.

AJ, Alex, Alexz, Austin, BP, Brittany, Burley, Celandra, C.J., Derrick, Destiny, Emily, Eric, **Eric and Colleen and Julie**, Evan, Hans, **Helen and Danny**, Imp, Informer, JC, Jessica, Jonathan, Josh, Julie, Justin, Kendra, Kevin, Kevin and Michaela, Kim, Krister, KS and CK, Laura, Lea Ann, Lloyd, Lori, Matt and Sylvia, Matthew, Megan, Melissa, Mike, M. L., Morgan, Nathan,

Nicky, Nix, Nusy, Olivia, Peter, Queenkoalaandme, RaeLynn, **Rosemary and Neil (FindingMickey.com)**, Ryan, Sandy, Sarah, Sawyer, Seeing, Scott, Serena, Shannon, Shaun, Stephanie, **Tamera**, Toneto and Laura and Steph, Ty, **Where's Mickey (myspace.com/where'smickey)**.

14

Read This First! • • • • • • • • •

My guess is that you have visited Disneyland before, perhaps many times. But if I've guessed wrong, and this is your first visit, then this note is for you.

Searching for Hidden Mickeys is lots of fun. But it's not a substitute for letting the magic of Disney sweep over you as you experience the Disneyland parks for the first time. For one thing, the scavenger hunts I present in this book do not include all the attractions at Disneyland. That's because some of them don't have Hidden Mickeys! For another, the first-time visitor should get ready for fun by also consulting a general Disneyland guidebook for descriptions of Disneyland attractions, shows, dining, and other tourist information.

That doesn't mean you can't search for Hidden Mickeys, too. Just follow the suggestions in Chapter One of this book for "Finding Hidden Mickeys Without Scavenger Hunting."

Hidden Mickey Mania

● ●

Have you ever marveled at a "Hidden Mickey"? People in the know often shout with glee when they recognize one. Some folks are so involved with discovering them that Hidden Mickeys can be visualized where none actually exist. These outbreaks of Hidden Mickey mania are confusing to the unenlightened. So let's get enlightened!

Here's the definition of an official Hidden Mickey: a partial or complete image of Mickey Mouse that has been hidden by Disney's Imagineers and artists in the designs of Disney attractions, hotels, restaurants, and other areas. These images are designed to blend into their surroundings. Sharp-eyed visitors have the fun of finding them.

The practice probably started as an inside joke among the Imagineers (the designers and builders of Disney attractions). According to Disney guru Jim Hill (www. JimHillMedia.com), Hidden Mickeys originated in the late 1970s or early 1980s, when Disney was building Epcot and management wanted to restrict Disney characters like Mickey and Minnie to Walt Disney World's Magic Kingdom. The Imagineers designing Epcot couldn't resist slipping Mickeys into the new park, and thus "Hidden Mickeys" were born. Guests and "Cast Members" (Disney employees) started spotting them and the concept took on a life of its own. Today, Hidden Mickeys are anticipated in any new Disney construction anywhere, and Hidden Mickey fans can't wait to find them.

Hidden Mickeys come in all sizes and many forms. The most common is an outline of Mickey's head formed by three intersecting circles, one for Mickey's round head and two for his round ears. Among Hidden Mickey fans, this image is known as the "classic" Hidden Mickey, a term I will adopt in this book. Other Hidden Mickeys include a side or oblique (usually three-quarter) profile of Mickey's face and head, a side profile of his entire body, a full-length silhouette of his body seen from the front, a detailed picture of his face or body, or a three-dimensional Mickey Mouse. Sometimes just his gloves, handprints, shoes, or ears appear. Even his name or initials in unusual places may qualify as a Hidden Mickey.

And it's not just Mickeys that are hidden. The term "Hidden Mickey" also applies to hidden images of other popular Characters. There are Hidden Minnies, Hidden Donald Ducks, Hidden Goofys, and other Hidden characters in the Disneyland Resort, and I include many of them in this book.

The sport of finding Hidden Mickeys is catching on and adds even more interest to an already fun-filled Disneyland vacation. This book is your "field guide" to more than 275 Hidden Mickeys in Disneyland. To add to the fun, instead of just describing them, I've organized them into three scavenger hunts, one for each of the theme parks and one for all the rest of the Disneyland Resort: Downtown Disney District, the resort hotels, and beyond. The hunts are designed for maximum efficiency so that you can spend your time looking for Mickey rather than cooling your heels in lines. Follow the Clues and you will find the best Hidden Mickeys Disneyland has to offer. If you have trouble spotting a particular Hidden Mickey (some are extraordinarily well camouflaged!) you can turn to the Hints at the end of each scavenger hunt for a fuller description.

Scavenger Hunting for Hidden Mickeys

To have the most fun and find the most Mickeys, follow these tips:

★ **Arrive early** for the theme park hunts, say 30 minutes before the official opening time. Pick up a Guidemap and Times Guide and plot your course. Then look for Hidden Mickeys in the waiting area while you wait for the rope to drop. You'll find the clues for those areas by checking the *Index to Mickey's Hiding Places* in the back of this book. Look under "Entrance areas." You'll notice that headliner attractions are the first stops in the scavenger hunts. If you arrive later in the day, you may want to pick up a FASTPASS for the first major attraction and then skip down a few clues to stay ahead of the crowds.

★ "Clues" and "Hints"

Clues under each attraction will guide you to the Hidden Mickey(s). If you have trouble spotting them, you can turn to the Hints at the end of the hunt for a fuller description. The Clues and Hints are numbered consecutively, that is, Hint 1 goes with Clue 1; so it's easy to find the right Hint if you need it. In some cases, *Soarin' Over California* in Disney's California Adventure for example, you may have to ride the attraction more than once to find all the Hidden Mickeys.

★ Scoring

All Hidden Mickeys are fun to find, but all Hidden Mickeys aren't the same. Some are easier to find than others. I assign point values to Hidden Mickeys, identifying them as easy to spot (a value of 1 point) to difficult to find the first time (5 points). I also consider the complexity and uniqueness of the image: the more complex or unique the Hidden Mickey, the higher the point value. For example, some of the easy-to-spot Hidden Mickeys in Mickey's Toontown in Disneyland are one- or two-point Mickeys. The brilliantly camouflaged Mickey hiding in the tree on one of the ceramic panels decorating a column outside Disney's Grand Californian Hotel is a five-pointer.

★ Playing the game

You can hunt solo or with others; competitively or just for fun. There's room to tally your score in the guide. Families with young children may want to focus on one- and two-point Mickeys that the little ones will have no trouble spotting. (Of course, little ones tend to be sharp-eyed, so they may spot familiar shapes before you do in some of the more complex patterns.) Or you may want to split your party into teams and see who can rack up the most points (in which case, you'll probably want to have a copy of this guide for each team).

Of course, you don't have to play the game at all. You can simply look for Hidden Mickeys in attractions as you come to them (see "Finding Hidden Mickeys Without Scavenger Hunting" below).

★ Following the clues

The hunts often call for crisscrossing the parks. This may seem illogical at first, but trust me, it will keep you ahead of the crowds. Besides, it adds to the fun of the hunt and, if you're playing competitively, keeps everyone on their toes.

★ Waiting in line

Don't waste time in lines. If the wait is longer than 15 minutes, get a FASTPASS (if available and you're eligible), move on to the next attraction, and then come back at your FASTPASS time. Alternatively, use the Singles Line if available. Exception: In some attractions, the Hidden Mickey(s) can only be seen from the Standby queue (the regular line), and not from the FASTPASS or Singles queues. (I've not suggested FASTPASS or Singles queues in the Clues section when that is the case.) The lines at these attractions should not be too long if you start your scavenger hunt when the park opens and follow the hunt clues as given. If you do encounter long lines, come back later during a parade or in the hour before the park closes.

★ Playing fair

Be considerate of other guests. Some Hidden Mickeys are in restaurants and shops. Ask a Cast Member's permission before searching inside sit-down restaurants, and avoid the busy mealtime hours unless you are one of the diners. Tell the Cast Members and other guests who see you looking around what you're up to, so they can share in the fun.

Finding Hidden Mickeys Without Scavenger Hunting

If scavenger hunts don't appeal to you, you don't have to use them. You can find Hidden Mickeys in the specific rides and other attractions you visit by using the *Index to Mickey's Hiding Places* in the back of this book. For easy lookup, attractions are also listed under their appropriate "lands" (for example, Frontierland in Disneyland and Hollywood Pictures Backlot in Disney's California Adventure). To find Hidden Mickeys in the attraction, restaurant, hotel, or shop you are visiting, turn to the *Index*, locate the appropriate page, and follow the Clue(s) to find the Hidden Mickey(s).

Caution: You won't find every Disneyland attraction, restaurant, hotel, or shop in the Index. Only those with confirmed Hidden Mickeys are included in this guide.

Hidden Mickeys: Real or Wishful Thinking?

The classic (three-circle) Mickeys are the most controversial, for good reason. Much debate surrounds the gathering of circular forms throughout Disneyland. The three cannonball craters in the wall of the fort in *Pirates of the Caribbean* (Clue 33 in the Disneyland Park Scavenger Hunt) is obviously the work of a clever artist. However, three-circle configurations occur spontaneously in art and nature, as in collections of grapes, tomatoes, pumpkins, bubbles, oranges, cannonballs, and the like. Unlike the cannonball crater Hidden Mickey in *Pirates of the Caribbean*, it may be difficult to attribute a random "classic Mickey" configuration of circles to a deliberate Imagineer design.

So which groupings of three circles qualify as Hidden Mickeys as opposed to wishful thinking? Unfortunately, no master list of actual or "Imagineer-approved" Hidden Mickeys exists. Purists demand that a true classic Hidden Mickey should have proper proportions and positioning. The round head must be larger than the ear circles (so that three equal circles in the proper alignment would not qualify as a Hidden Mickey). The head and ears must be touching and in perfect position for Mickey's head and ears.

On the other hand, Disney's recent mantra is: "If the guest thinks it's a Hidden Mickey, then by golly it is one!" Of course, I appreciate Disney's respect for their guests' opinions. However, when the subject is Hidden Mickeys, let's apply some guidelines. My own criteria are looser than the purist's but stricter than the "anything goes" Disney approach. I prefer to use a few sensible guidelines.

To be classified as a genuine classic Hidden Mickey, the three circles should satisfy the following criteria:

1. Purposeful (sometimes you can sense that the circles were placed on purpose).

2. Proportionate sizes (head larger than the ears and somewhat proportionate to the ears).

3. Round or at least "roundish."

4. The ears don't touch each other, and the ears are above the head (not beside it).

5. The ears touch the head or they're close to touching.

6. The grouping of circles is exceptional or unique in appearance.

7. The circles are hidden or somewhat hidden and not obviously décor (decorative).

Having spelled out some ground rules, allow me now to bend them in one instance. Some Hidden Mickeys are sentimental favorites with Disney fans, even though they may actually represent "wishful thinking." (My neighbor, Lew Brooks, calls them "two-beer" Mickeys.) Who am I to defy tradition? For example, the three circles on the back of the turtle in *Snow White's Scary Adventures* (Clue 100 in the Disneyland Scavenger Hunt) form a not-quite-proportionate "classic" Mickey. However, if you ask Cast Members near this attraction about a Hidden Mickey, they'll whisper to you these cryptic words: "Watch for the turtle!"

Hidden Mickeys vs. Decorative Mickeys

Some Mickeys are truly hidden, not visible to the tourist. They may be located behind the scenes, available only to Cast

Members. You won't find them in this field. I only include Hidden Mickeys that are accessible the guest. Other Mickeys are decorative; they were placed in plain sight to enhance the décor. For example, in a restaurant, I consider a pat of butter shaped like Mickey Mouse to be a decorative (aka décor) Mickey. Disneyland is loaded with decorative Mickeys. You'll find images of Mickey Mouse on items ranging from manhole covers, to laundry room soap dispensers, to toilet paper wrappers and shower curtains in the hotels. I do not include these ubiquitous and sometimes changing images in this book unless they are unique or hard to spot.

Hidden Mickeys can change or be accidentally removed over time, by the processes of nature or by the continual cleaning and refurbishing that goes on at Disneyland. For example, a classic Mickey on an outside duct at *MuppetVision 3-D* was painted over and is no longer with us. Cast Members themselves sometimes create or remove Hidden Mickeys.

My Selection Process

I trust you've concluded by now that Hidden Mickey Science is an evolving specialty. Which raises the question, how did I choose the more than 275 Hidden Mickeys in the scavenger hunts in this guide? I compiled my list of Hidden Mickeys from all the resources to which I had access: my own sightings, sightings sent to me by others (see "Acknowledgements"), websites, books, and Cast Members. (Cast members in each specific area usually — but not always! — know where some Hidden Mickeys are located.) Then I embarked on my verification hunts, asking for help along the way from generous Disney Cast Members. I have included only those Hidden Mickeys I could personally verify.

Furthermore, some Hidden Mickeys are visible only intermittently or only from certain vantage points in ride vehicles. I don't generally include these Mickeys, unless I feel that adequate descriptions will allow anyone to find them. So the scavenger hunts include only those images I believe to be recognizable as Hidden Mickeys and visible to the general touring guest. It is quite likely, though, that one or more of the Hidden Mickeys described in this book will disappear over time.

I'll try to let you know when I discover that a Hidden Mickey has disappeared for good by posting the information on my website:

www.HiddenMickeysGuide.com

If you find one missing before I do, I hope you'll let me know by emailing me care of my website. Just hit the "Contact" button at the top of my home page and drop me a note.

I have enjoyed finding each and every Hidden Mickey in this book. I'm certain I'll find more as time goes by, and I hope you can spot new Hidden Mickeys during your visit.

So put on some comfortable walking shoes and experience Disneyland like you never have before!

Happy Hunting!

— *Steve Barrett*

CHAPTER 2

Disneyland Park Scavenger Hunt

★ Arrive at the entrance turnstiles (with your admission ticket) 30 to 40 minutes before the official opening time.

Clue 1: At the security bag check area, study the signs above you for a classic Mickey on a key chain.
4 points

Clue 2: Now search the signs again for a classic Mickey on a ride vehicle.
4 points

Clue 3: As soon as you pass through the entrance turnstile, look around for a classic Mickey.
3 points

Clue 4: Inside the entrance, glance upwards for a classic Mickey on a sign.
3 points

★ Go to **Space Mountain** in Tomorrowland.

Clue 5: Find Mickey along the entrance queue.
2 points

Clue 6: See anything on the ride vehicles?
2 points

Clue 7: During the ride, watch the space objects above you for a Hidden Mickey.
4 points

★ Go to **Buzz Lightyear Astro Blasters**.

Clue 8: Search for two Mickey continents along the entrance queue.
3 points for each one; 6 points total

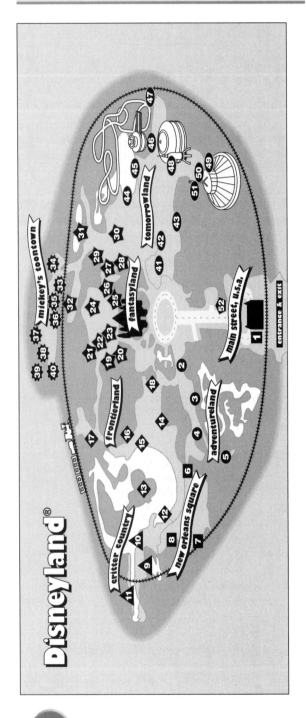

1 Disneyland Railroad, Entrance

● adventureland
2 Enchanted Tiki Room
3 Jungle Cruise
4 Tarzan's Treehouse™
5 Indiana Jones™ Adventure

■ new orleans square
6 Pirates of the Caribbean
7 Disneyland Railroad
8 Haunted Mansion

◄ critter country
9 Splash Mountain
10 Davy Crockett's Explorer Canoes
11 The Many Adventures of Winnie the Pooh

◆ frontierland
12 Rafts to Tom Sawyer Island
13 Pirate's Lair on Tom Sawyer Island
14 The Golden Horseshoe Stage
15 Mark Twain Riverboat and Sailing Ship Columbia
16 Big Thunder Mountain Railroad
17 Big Thunder Ranch
18 Frontierland Shootin' Exposition

★ fantasyland
19 Pinocchio's Daring Journey
20 Snow White's Scary Adventures
21 Casey Jr. Circus Train
22 King Arthur Carrousel
23 Sleeping Beauty Castle Walkthrough
24 Dumbo the Flying Elephant
25 Peter Pan's Flight
26 Mr. Toad's Wild Ride
27 Mad Tea Party
28 Alice in Wonderland
29 Storybook Land Canal Boats
30 Matterhorn Bobsleds
31 "it's a small world"
32 Fantasyland Theatre

✹ mickey's toontown
33 Disneyland Railroad
34 Roger Rabbit's Car Toon Spin
35 Goofy's Playhouse
36 Donald's Boat
37 Minnie's House
38 Mickey's House
39 Chip 'n Dale Treehouse
40 Gadget's Go Coaster

● tomorrowland
41 Astro Orbitor
42 Buzz Lightyear Astro Blasters
43 Star Tours
44 Finding Nemo Submarine Voyage
45 Disneyland Monorail
46 Autopia
47 Disneyland Railroad
48 Innoventions
49 Space Mountain
50 "Honey, I Shrunk the Audience"
51 Starcade

⬡ main street, u.s.a.
52 Main Street Cinema

27

Clue 9: Find two classic (three-circle) Hidden Mickeys along the entrance queue.
3 points for each one; 6 points total

Clue 10: On the ride, watch to your left for a classic Mickey on a block.
3 points

Clue 11: After you step off the ride vehicle, search for a side-profile Mickey on the wall.
2 points

Clue 12: Find two classic Mickeys in this same mural.
2 points each; 4 total

★ Go to the **elevator for the Disneyland Monorail**, which is near both the monorail exit and *Finding Nemo Submarine Voyage*.

Clue 13: Search carefully for a Hidden Mickey near the elevator.
5 points

★ Walk toward the **Matterhorn Bobsleds** in Fantasyland.

Clue 14: Search the mountain for Mickey.
4 points

Clue 15: Study the right *Bobsleds* queue area for a Hidden Mickey on a coat of arms.
4 points

★ Now ride **Peter Pan's Flight**.

Clue 16: At the beginning of the ride, read two names in blocks below you.
4 points for finding both

Clue 17: Look for Mickey in Big Ben.
5 points

★ Walk to **Big Thunder Mountain Railroad** in Frontierland.

Clue 18: While on the ride, search for three gears that form a classic Mickey.
3 points

Clue 19: Find Mickey at the exit.
3 points

★ Cross the park to Critter Country. Get a FASTPASS for *Splash Mountain,* then stroll over to **The Many Adventures of Winnie the Pooh**.

Clue 20: Study the "Hunny Pot" vehicles for a classic Mickey.
2 points

Clue 21: Just after the ride starts, be aware of a classic Mickey in the wood.
4 points

Clue 22: Look for classic Mickey circles near Heffa-lumps.
3 points

★ Walk to Adventureland and join the Standby queue (the regular line) for **Indiana Jones™ Adventure**.

Clue 23: Study the walls of the queue for Mickey's "initials."
4 points

Clue 24: In the circular room with the rope you can pull on, search for a stone disk (propped upright) with a tiny classic Mickey.
5 points

Clue 25: Now look up for a classic Mickey in the same room.
4 points

Clue 26: Find a large classic Mickey in the room with the video screen.
4 points

Clue 27: Toward the end of the video room, look up and say hi to Eeyore!
5 points

Clue 28: When you leave the video room, peer into an office to spot Mickey.
3 points

Clue 29: After the ride starts, gaze up into Mara's huge face for a classic Mickey.
3 points

Clue 30: When your vehicle enters the Mummy Room, find a Mickey Mouse hat.
5 points

★ Wander over to New Orleans Square and hop on *Pirates of the Caribbean*.

Clue 31: Check out the Mickey on Davy Jones.
5 points

Clue 32: Stay alert for Mickey on the beach!
3 points

Clue 33: On the ride, in the first fight scene, spot a classic Mickey on a wall.
5 points

Clue 34: Near the end of the ride, find a classic Mickey on armor.
4 points

Clue 35: After you exit the boat, look around for a classic Mickey on a door.
2 points

★ Turn left at the exit to enjoy *Haunted Mansion*.

Clue 36: Look high along the mansion walls for a Hidden Mickey.
3 points

Clue 37: Search for Mickey in the wallpaper.
3 points

Clue 38: While on the ride, can you find Donald Duck?
4 points

Clue 39: As you ride, keep alert for plates and saucers.
3 points

Clue 40: Look for a clock with a Hidden Mickey in the attic.
5 points

★ Mosey on over to **The Golden Horseshoe** in Frontierland. You can order a counter-service lunch and, if the timing is right, catch a great show (check your Times Guide).

Clue 41: Check around the stage for a classic Mickey.
3 points

★ Enter the **Pioneer Mercantile shop**.

Clue 42: Examine the wall for Mickey.
3 points

★ Ride **Mark Twain Riverboat** or **Sailing Ship Columbia**.

Clue 43: While on the boat, scour the river for a classic Mickey in the water.
3 points

Clue 44: Seek out the **Mark Twain Riverboat** (if you haven't already). Concentrate on the front of the boat to spot a Hidden Mickey.
2 points

Clue 45: Search for Mickey Mouse in a painting near the *Mark Twain Riverboat* loading dock.
4 points

★ Float on the **Raft to Tom Sawyer Island**.

Clue 46: On Tom Sawyer Island, seek out a cavern entrance with a classic Mickey.
3 points

Clue 47: Climb up into the first treehouse you find and look outside and down for a classic Mickey.
4 points

★ Return by raft to Frontierland. Turn right and walk to the **Briar Patch store** (near *Splash Mountain*).

Clue 48: Look inside the store for a Hidden Mickey.
3 points

★ Ride **Splash Mountain** with your FASTPASS.

Clue 49: Check out the outside entrance queue for a tiny Mickey.
5 points

Clue 50: Search for a classic Mickey along the inside queue.
3 points

Clue 51: While on the ride, stay alert for a picture of Mickey on the wall.
4 points

★ Stroll to **Big Thunder Ranch**.

Clue 52: Spot a Hidden Mickey near the entrance.
4 points

★ Cross the central hub to Tomorrowland. Ride **Autopia** or get a FASTPASS to ride later if the Standby line wait is more than 15 to 20 minutes.

Clue 53: While in line or on the ride, find a classic Mickey on the cars.
3 points

★ Check into **Star Tours**. Watch the pre-boarding video. You can skip the actual simulator ride if you want, or indulge yourself in space travel Disney-style!

Clue 54: Search for a Hidden Mickey in the pre-boarding video.
3 points

★ Make time in your schedule for the **afternoon parade**.

(Note: The parade floats change from time to time but usually have Hidden Mickeys as part of their decoration.) The antique Grand Marshal automobile sometimes leads the parade.

Clue 55: Search this antique car for several Hidden Mickeys.
5 bonus points for spotting three or more

★ In Adventureland, line up for the **Jungle Cruise**.

Clue 56: From the waiting queue, look for a Hidden Mickey on one of the boats.
5 points

★ If you're up for a mild climb through an imaginative tree, check out **Tarzan's Treehouse** in Adventureland.

Clue 57: Study the room with the ship's wheel for a Hidden Mickey near the floor.
3 points

Clue 58: In this same room, look for a Hidden Mickey on the wall.
3 points

Clue 59: Along your walk through the tree, characters from *Beauty and the Beast* make an appearance.
4 points for spotting both

Clue 60: Watch for a classic Mickey made of "drums."
3 points

★ Walk back across the central hub and through Fantasyland to **Mickey's Toontown** (or hop on the *Disneyland Railroad Train* at New Orleans Square).

(Note: You'll find many Mickey shapes throughout Toontown. I don't include the larger, more obvious Mickey images as Hidden Mickeys; they're more properly designated "décor" Mickeys.)

Clue 61: Look for Mickey near the entrance to Mickey's Toontown.
2 points

★ Get in line for **Gadget's Go Coaster**. The Hidden Mickeys are along the queue. You can skip the actual ride if you want; just ask to exit when you reach the loading area.

Clue 62: Stay alert for at least three rock classic Mickeys in the queue walls.
3 points each; 9 total

Clue 63: Gaze around the vehicle loading area for a Hidden Mickey.
4 points

★ Stroll over to **Mickey's House**.

Clue 64: See anything in his front door?
1 point

Clue 65: Glance down for Mickey.
1 point

Clues 66 and 67: Look inside a glass-fronted bookcase for several Hidden Mickeys.
3 points apiece for one on each of two books

Clue 68: Stare at other books in the first room.
3 points

Clues 69 and 70: In the piano room, search for two Hidden Mickeys in a bookcase.
2 points for each one

Clues 71, 72, and 73: Find some Hidden Characters in the piano.
2 points for a Hidden Mickey
3 points each for two other Characters; 8 points total

Clue 74: Something's atop the piano.
2 points

Clue 75: Pay attention to a special mirror inside Mickey's Movie Barn (the room in *Mickey's House* where you wait to meet Mickey in person).
4 points

Clue 76: Also in Mickey's Movie Barn, watch the countdown on the film screen.
4 points

Clue 77: Once outside, admire Mickey's car and find a Hidden Mickey.
3 points

Clue 78: Search for Mickey on a lamp.
3 points

★ Saunter over to **Minnie's House**.

Clue 79: Mickey is hiding in the first room inside.
3 points

Clue 80: Mickey is hiding in Minnie's kitchen.
2 points

★ Search for Mickey outside *Minnie's House*.

Clue 81: Look near the big blue doors.
5 points

★ Locate the **telephone hut** near *Minnie's House*.

Clue 82: Find Mickey in the small building with the telephones.
2 points

★ If you're in Mickey's Toontown when **Clarabelle's Frozen Yogurt** closes, look around for a Hidden Mickey. (Ask a Cast Member about closing time; you may need to return later.)

Clue 83: At closing, a Hidden Mickey appears.
2 points

Clue 84: Find two more at the **Post Office**.
4 points total for spotting both

★ Walk or take the *Disneyland Railroad Train* to Tomorrowland. Go to **Innoventions**.

Clue 85: Just after you enter the building, check out Tom Morrow for a Hidden Mickey.
4 points

★ Enjoy the **Dream Home**, and spot a few Hidden Mickeys.

Clue 86: Don't miss Mickey at the front door!
3 points

Clue 87: Mickey is also just inside the front door.
3 points

Clue 88: Look down for Mickey as you walk through the Dream Home.
2 points

Clue 89: Now check out the murals for classic Mickeys.
4 points

Clue 90: Study a wall in the **ASIMO robot show area** for a Hidden Mickey.
3 points

Clue 91: Find Mickey near the computer in the ASIMO show area.
3 points

Clue 92: Watch the ASIMO show video for a Hidden Mickey.
4 points

★ Exit *Innoventions*.

Clue 93: Study the murals on the rotating outside walls for two Hidden Mickeys.
4 points total for finding both

Clue 94: Now study the rotating murals for another Hidden Character.
4 points

★ Walk back to Fantasyland, and get in line for **Mr. Toad's Wild Ride**.

Clue 95: Find a tiny Mickey along the entrance queue.
4 points

Clue 96: At the beginning of the ride, stare at a right-hand door for a tiny dark classic Mickey on the glass of the door.
5 points

Clue 97: Search for Mickey in beer foam.
4 points

★ Next ride **Alice in Wonderland**.

Clue 98: On the ride, search for a classic Mickey in red paint.
4 points

★ Go to **Snow White's Scary Adventures**.

Clue 99: Find Mickey at the loading dock.
3 points

Clue 100: On the ride, watch for a classic Mickey on an animal.
3 points

★ Go next door to **Pinocchio's Daring Journey**.

Clue 101: Watch the floor for a yellow Hidden Mickey.
4 points

Clue 102: Look for a Hidden Mickey near a ship.
5 points

★ Grab a bite to eat if you're hungry. Try the Village Haus Restaurant for a quick bite (or any other eatery that's not too crowded). If you choose the Village Haus Restaurant, check out Clues 106 and 107.

★ Amble over to **Casey Jr. Circus Train**.

Clue 103: Examine the conductor's cabin for Mickey.
3 points

★ Relax on a gentle boat ride at *"it's a small world."*

Clue 104: Watch the ceiling for a Hidden Mickey.
3 points

★ Stroll over to the **King Arthur Carrousel**. Find the Hidden Mickeys from outside the Carrousel first, then ride if you wish.

Clue 105: Check out the horses for several Hidden Mickeys.
2 points each; 6 points total

★ Take a short hike over to the **Village Haus Restaurant**.

Clue 106: Search for Mickey in the restaurant. (Psst! It's "sitting" on the floor.)
3 points

Clue 107: Look for a Hidden Mickey near the ceiling.
5 points

★ Cross Fantasyland to the **Mad Hatter shop**, not far from the Mad Tea Party attraction.

Clue 108: Search around inside the shop for a Hidden cat.
5 points

Clue 109: Spot Hidden Mickeys outside the shop.
2 points for each of two Hidden Mickeys; 4 points total

★ Back near Sleeping Beauty Castle, locate the **Castle Heraldry Shoppe**.

Clue 110: Look for two Hidden Mickeys outside the store.
5 points for finding both of them

★ Walk to the rear of Tomorrowland to **Redd Rockett's Pizza Port**.

Clue 111: Search around inside the restaurant for a Hidden Mickey.
3 points

★ Retrace your steps to **The Star Trader shop** (not far from *Star Tours*).

Clue 112: Glance inside the store for small classic Mickeys.
2 points

★ Cross the central hub to reach the **walkway to Frontierland**.

Clue 113: Look for a Hidden Mickey along the entrance walkway to Frontierland.
3 points

★ Go left to the **River Belle Terrace** restaurant.

Clue 114: Find a Hidden Mickey in the restaurant.
3 points

★ Go to **Main Street, U.S.A.** to find more Hidden Mickeys!

Clue 115: Check out inside the **Plaza Inn** for a Hidden Mickey.
3 points

★ Stand outside the **Silhouette Studio**.

Clue 116: Spot a Hidden Mickey in a display window.
4 points

★ Enter the **Gibson Girl Ice Cream Parlor**.

Clue 117: Look up for a Hidden Mickey.
2 points

★ Walk over to **Blue Ribbon Bakery**.

Clue 118: Study the walls inside the bakery for a Hidden Mickey.
3 points

Clue 119: Find a Hidden Mickey on a **fruit cart**.
4 points

Clue 120: Enter the **Market House** and search the wall for a Hidden Mickey.
3 points

★ Stroll down Main Street to **Main Street Cinema**. Walk inside.

Clue 121: Look around for some Hidden Mickeys.
3 points

Clue 122: Outside Main Street Cinema, search for two more Hidden Mickeys.
2 points apiece; 4 points total

Clue 123: Don't miss the small Hidden Mickey on a game machine inside the **Penny Arcade**!
4 points

★ Walk to the Rivers of America in Frontierland and watch the **Fantasmic!** show for a Hidden Mickey.

Clue 124: Be alert for a Hidden Mickey on the water screen.
5 points

★ Don't miss the nighttime **fireworks show**!

Clue 125: Watch the sky during the fireworks show for a Hidden Mickey.
5 points

★ Exit Disneyland Park and look around the **entrance plaza** for two more kinds of Hidden Mickeys.

Clue 126: Look for Mickey at your feet.
3 points

Clue 127: Spot Mickey on poles.
3 points

Total Points for Disneyland Park =

How'd You Do?

Up to 178 points – Bronze
179 to 354 points – Silver
355 points and over – Gold
444 points – Perfect Score

(If you earned bonus points by spotting Hidden Mickeys on the Grand Marshal's car during the afternoon parade, you may have done even better.)

Notes

**Caution:
Don't peek at this
section unless you
really want help!**

Entrance area

Hint 1: In the security bag check area, various pictures of characters from *The Lion King* hang above you. On the picture with the warning "Hold On To Your Gear!" a small key chain flies through the air behind Timon and Pumbaa on a roller coaster. A tiny black classic Mickey is on the blue part of the key chain. (You may need to wander around the security area to find the picture.)

Hint 2: Also in the security bag check area, on the sign warning "Let The Cubs Decide If They Want To Ride," a small white classic Mickey is above the word "Cubs" on a blue ride vehicle occupied by Timon and Pumbaa.

Hint 3: As soon as you enter Disneyland, turn around to spot the classic Mickey speaker grid on the utility box next to the entrance turnstile. The ticket attendant may be blocking your view.

HINTS HINTS HINTS HINTS HINTS HINTS HINTS HINTS HINTS HINTS HINTS HINTS HINTS

Hint 4: Inside the entrance to the right, the sign for "Strollers & Wheelchairs" has classic Mickeys at either side in the scrollwork.

Tomorrowland

- Space Mountain

Hint 5: Mickey ears appear on the right side of the safety video in which you're asked to place "loose possessions in the storage pouch in front of you."

Hint 6: The speakers on the back of the ride vehicle seats form classic Mickeys.

Hint 7: About one-third of the way along the ride, three asteroids flying to the upper right of your vehicle form a slightly distorted classic Mickey.

- Buzz Lightyear Astro Blasters

Hint 8: As soon as you enter the building, look for two "Ska-densii" planets with side-profile "continent" Mickeys along the right side wall.

Hint 9: Two upside-down classic Mickeys appear in the large "Planets of the Galactic Alliance" mural on the wall of the entrance queue. One is located at about 10:00 in the planet named K'lifooel'ch and is made of small green spheres. The other is made of white spheres and hides on the right side of the mural above the words "K'tleendon Kan Cluster."

Hint 10: A classic Mickey is etched on a block in the first show room to the left of the vehicle, just past a large rotating wheel and left of a row of target batteries.

Hint 11: Another side-profile Mickey is on a "Ska-densii" planet's continent on a right wall mural across from the photo viewing area. If it looks familiar, it's because you see the same Hidden Mickeys (as well as the two below) on an entrance-queue mural.

44

Hint 12: On this same mural on the right wall along the inside exit, a classic Mickey lies along the outer edge of the K'lifooel'ch planet of spheres at about the "10 o'clock" location (other classic Mickey spheres are in this planet) and an upside-down classic Mickey is formed by three white spheres at the middle right of the mural, above the words "K'tleendon Kan Cluster."

- near the elevator for the Disneyland monorail

Hint 13: A classic Mickey impression is in the rock wall about one foot off the floor and between two separated handrails.

Fantasyland

- Matterhorn Bobsleds

Hint 14: A large black classic Mickey hole is in the side of the Matterhorn mountain. You can see it from various vantage points in Tomorrowland.

Hint 15: A tiny black classic Mickey is in the middle of a red and white coat of arms at the rear of the right queue. The Mickey is on a red triangle at the bottom of a white pole.

- Peter Pan's Flight

Hint 16: As you walk through the entrance queue, lean over the rail and look into the first scene (the bedroom) of the ride. Alphabet blocks are stacked and scattered on the floor. On the ride, as your vehicle soars over the bedroom, look down at the blocks and find these words: "DISNEY" spelled as "D13NEY," and "PETER PAN."

(Note: Cast Members may change these blocks around at times.)

Hint 17: As you fly over London, a side-view Mickey silhouette hides in a top window on the left side of Big Ben. Look back at the window as you pass by the clock tower.

Frontierland

- Big Thunder Mountain Railroad

Hint 18: As you start to climb the second hill, look to your left, near the bottom of the hill, for three gears that form a large, upside-down classic Mickey.

Hint 19: On your right as you exit, the highest three green lobes in the cactus garden form an oval classic Mickey. At times, other collections of cactus lobes may also form Mickeys.

Critter Country

- The Many Adventures of Winnie the Pooh

Hint 20: The back and lower legs of the "Heffabee" on top of each ride vehicle form an upside-down classic Mickey.

Hint 21: In the first part of the entrance tunnel, a small, classic Hidden Mickey is on tree bark to the right of your vehicle, at about eye level.

Hint 22: Near the end of the ride, there is a Heffalump collage on your right. Look in the bottom right-hand corner for a classic Mickey.

Adventureland

- Indiana Jones™ Adventure

Hint 23: Across from the first drinking fountains in the inside Standby queue, Mickey's initials "M M" in "Maraglyphics" appear on the left wall, just above a horizontal crack in the wall.

Hint 24: On the side of a bamboo structure just opposite the hanging rope, a large painted stone disk has a tiny classic Hidden Mickey symbol on the lower right edge of the outer circle of symbols.

Hint 25: On the ceiling, Mara's giant nose is a classic Mickey.

Hint 26: When you enter the room showing the video on a screen, study the left wall for a large classic Hidden Mickey between the last two lights on the wall.

Hint 27: *Indiana Jones Adventure* was built over a previous Eeyore (Cast Member) parking lot. As a tribute to the past, an original white parking sign shaped as Eeyore was placed in the video room, high up in the rafters. At the end of the video room, turn around and look up, to the left of the projector. If you don't spot it, ask a nearby Cast Member to help you find it.

Hint 28: In an office just past the video room, Mickey and Minnie Mouse are pictured on a partially visible magazine page. The magazine is on a desktop.

Hint 29: Shortly after the ride starts, look at Mara's face for a (not quite perfect) classic Mickey formed by the curves of the nostrils and the oval depression just below the middle of the nose.

Hint 30: As soon as your vehicle turns a corner and enters the Mummy Room, look left for a skeleton wearing a Mickey Mouse hat. Let's hope the hat stays put!

New Orleans Square

- Pirates of the Caribbean

Hint 31: As Davy Jones appears in the mist in front of your boat, three circles on the lower left front of his hat (to your left) form a tiny classic Mickey.

Hint 32: After the second drop, look to the right to spot shells on the beach that form a classic Mickey. Look for the beach scene with the skeletons and the moving crab.

Hint 33: In the first battle scene, there are three cannonball impact craters on the upper part of the fort wall on the right side of your boat. This crater classic Mickey is below the middle cannon and best seen if you turn around to view it as you are passing by the fort.

Hint 34: This classic Mickey is in the last room, where two pieces of armor (chest plates) hang from the wall to the left of your boat. The gold armor, closest to the ride exit, has a coat of arms emblem. In the center of that emblem are classic Mickey circles.

Hint 35: On the right side as you exit, and before you reach the street outside, a classic Mickey-shaped lock adorns a back door to the Pieces of Eight shop.

- Haunted Mansion

Hint 36: As soon as you walk through the front door along the entrance queue, go to any of the candlestick holders on the wall. With your back to the wall, look up from underneath to enjoy a classic Mickey effect.

Hint 37: Large circles form classic Mickeys in the wall-paper of the Art Gallery after you exit the Stretching Room.

Hint 38: As you pass by the "endless hallway," check out the back of the purple chair for an abstract Donald Duck. Near the top of the chair, you can see his cap, which sits above his distorted eyes, face, and bill. (Note that the chair may change locations at times).

Hint 39: During the Ballroom scene, look down at the place settings near the center of the dining table. You'll see two small saucers and one larger plate forming a classic Mickey. The Cast Members move this Hidden Mickey around at times.

Hint 40: After the ballroom scene, look to the right as soon as you enter the attic. Find the clock on a bureau to the right of the round portrait of a bride and groom and just to the right of a bright orange and blue lamp. A brown classic Mickey hides behind the pendulum of the clock.

Frontierland

- The Golden Horseshoe

Hint 41: Walk toward the front of the stage and find a vent grate in the center of the lower front wall. Start at the lower right hole in the grate, and then look up and diagonally left one hole to a classic Mickey hole in the grate.

- Pioneer Mercantile shop

Hint 42: On the walls inside the Pioneer Mercantile gift shop, white river rocks at the lower center of some of the lamp covers form classic Mickeys.

- Mark Twain Riverboat / Sailing Ship Columbia

Hint 43: While boating on the Rivers of America, look out for three boulders in the water that form a classic Mickey. These boulders are on the right side of the ship near the shore of Tom Sawyer Island and across the river from an Indian scene.

Hint 44: Study the metal grillwork between the smokestacks and high above the *Mark Twain Riverboat*'s prow for a sideways classic Mickey.

Hint 45: To the right of the entrance for the *Mark Twain Riverboat* is a "Shipping Office." A painting advertising river excursions on the "Mark Twain" hangs on an 'office' wall. In the painting, Mickey Mouse is one of the passengers on the lowest deck.

- Tom Sawyer Island

Hint 46: As you exit the raft onto the island, turn left and look above the first cavern entrance you encounter. A classic Mickey depression is in the rock over the entrance.

Hint 47: Climb into the treehouse and look toward the Rivers of America. A classic, smiling Mickey is etched onto the top, horizontal cover of a short chimney.

- Briar Patch store

Hint 48: A classic Mickey made from heads of lettuce sits on an upper shelf over the front window inside the Briar Patch store.

- Splash Mountain

Hint 49: A tiny classic Mickey is formed of indentations in a protruding knot on a post at the beginning of the outside Standby entrance queue. Mickey is on the post just below the *Splash Mountain* Warning sign. You can also spot this Mickey as you exit *Haunted Mansion*.

Hint 50: As you enter the inside part of the entrance queue, look along the left side for a three-gear classic Mickey.

Hint 51: A framed photo of Mickey Mouse (riding in a *Splash Mountain* log) is on the upper wall to the left of your log, after the big drop and near the end of the ride.

- Big Thunder Ranch

Hint 52: At the entrance/exit, a classic Mickey formed by holes in the wood is under the soap dispenser next to the hand-washing station.

Tomorrowland

- Autopia

Hint 53: A black classic Mickey is in the upper right corner of the car license plates.

- Star Tours

Hint 54: While waiting to board the ride, watch the introductory video for an Ewok maneuvering to his seat on the shuttle. He's carrying a small, plush Mickey Mouse doll.

Afternoon Parade

Hint 55: On the Grand Marshal automobile, an attractive replica of an antique touring car, Classic Mickeys adorn the tires, the front bumper, the hood ornament, the nuts at the side of the front windshield, the tread on the spare tire on the rear of the car, and the brackets holding the spare tire in place.

Adventureland

- Jungle Cruise

Hint 56: Wait for the boat named Suwanee Lady. A rust-colored classic Mickey hides inside a frying pan hanging high from the middle of the port (far) side of the boat.

- Tarzan's Treehouse

Hint 57: Look for a trunk on the floor near the ship's wheel. The gold metal plate where the trunk's keyhole is located includes a classic Mickey made of round metal pieces. One of them encircles the keyhole.

Hint 58: Behind the ship's wheel, the far right curtain knobs at the right rear of the room form a classic Mickey. The curtain knobs directly to the left resemble a classic Mickey as well.

Hint 59: Pots that resemble Mrs. Potts and Chip from the *Beauty and the Beast* movie sit alongside the trail near the end.

Hint 60: Toward the end of the trail, three hollow drums or pots are arranged to form a classic Mickey.

Mickey's Toontown

- near the entrance

Hint 61: A white silhouette of Mickey's face and ears, seen from the front, adorns the

"Order of Mouse" seal on the overhead bridge to the left of the "Welcome to Mickey's Toontown" sign.

- Gadget's Go Coaster

Hint 62: These classic Mickeys aren't perfectly proportioned, but they seem purposeful.
  - The first is at the first turn to the left in the entrance queue.
  - The second is across from a bonsai tree and before the last right turn.
  - The third is a somewhat distorted classic Mickey, facing sideways, at the end of the wall on the left and about 20 feet before the boarding area.

Hint 63: Inside the loading area, turn around and locate the only blueprint on the rear wall. A partial drawing of Mickey Mouse is on the right side of the blueprint. Under Mickey are the words "DOG & PONY FOR MICKEY AT 4 PM."

- approaching and in Mickey's House

Hint 64: The window in Mickey's green front door is a partial classic Mickey.

Hint 65: The welcome mat at Mickey's front door is shaped like a classic Mickey.

Hint 66: As you enter the first room, stop by the green, glass-fronted bookcase. At the top of the spine of the book *2001: A Mouse Odyssey* are two yellow classic Mickeys.

Hint 67: In the same bookcase, find the book *See You Next Squeak*. You'll find a classic Mickey at the bottom of its spine.

Hint 68: At the left side of the first room, the bottom of the spine of the blue book entitled *My Fair Mouse* sports a classic Mickey.

Hint 69: Just as you enter the piano room, study the bookcase on the right side. The book *My Life with Walt* has a pink classic Mickey at the top of the spine.

- ASIMO robot show area

Hint 90: A small black classic Mickey is at the lower part of a painting on a wall of the ASIMO stage.

Hint 91: On the ASIMO show stage, a Mickey doll is on the desk next to the computer monitor.

Hint 92: When the lady talks to her husband over the videophone, a side view of Mickey is on the wall behind the husband.

- outside Innoventions

Hint 93: Among the items in the Entertainment section of the rotating wall murals outside is a black classic Mickey on a video monitor. In another mural, a large classic Mickey is on a blue wall, partially hidden behind a red monitor screen.

Hint 94: Also on the outside rotating murals, find a globe on a pedestal. The "continents" on the globe are shaped like Goofy, looking to the right.

Fantasyland

- Mr. Toad's Wild Ride

Hint 95: On the large statue of Mr. Toad, to the left of the inside entrance queue, a tiny red classic Mickey is at the lower part of his right cornea (above the white of the eye). It's in the left eye as you face the statue.

Hint 96: At the beginning of the ride, on the second set of doors that your car drives through, a tiny dark classic Mickey hides in the lower left part of the glass panel of the door on your right. This Mickey is hard to spot!

Hint 97: In Winky's Pub, about halfway through the ride, an upside-down classic Mickey appears in the foam in the top left corner of the left mug (as you face the scene) above Winky's hand.

- Alice in Wonderland

Hint 98: When the cards are "painting the roses red," look on the ground under the tree to the left for a slightly distorted classic Mickey. It's on a third-level ledge under the right hand with the paint brush and just to the left of a green heart.

- Snow White's Scary Adventures

Hint 99: A somewhat distorted classic Mickey is formed by bushes in the mural directly in front of your ride vehicle at the loading area. Look at the right end of the row of green bushes just past the rocky hill and to the left of the blue stream.

Hint 100: Early in the ride, look for the green turtle climbing stairs to the left of the ride vehicle. The large circle on the left side of the turtle shell forms the "head" of a three-circle classic Mickey.

- Pinocchio's Daring Journey

Hint 101: When your vehicle enters the Pleasure Island room, study the ground in front of the popcorn stand on your right. Some "spilled" popcorn forms a classic Hidden Mickey.

Hint 102: Near the end of the ride a big case holds a model ship. The middle of the top frame of the case is decorated with a wooden classic Mickey.

- Casey Jr. Circus Train

Hint 103: In the middle of the control panel at the front of the conductor's cabin, three round dials form a classic Mickey. You can spot this Mickey from the entrance area, so you can skip the ride if you want.

- "it's a small world"

Hint 104: In the last room of the ride, shadows from the last set of small balloons that move up and down at times form classic Mickeys to the left of your boat.

- King Arthur Carrousel

Hint 105: Find the golden horse, Jingles. Classic Mickeys made of gemstones are on the front and back of the horse. These classic Mickeys aren't perfectly proportioned and the 'ears' and 'head' aren't touching, but they seem purposeful.

- Village Haus Restaurant

Hint 106: Classic Mickey cutouts adorn the backs of a few of the children's highchairs.

Hint 107: In the dining room to the left as you walk through the main entrance, a light brown classic Mickey is on the stern of a sailing ship that sits on a shelf near the ceiling.

- Mad Hatter shop

Hint 108: Every few minutes, a faint image of the Cheshire Cat appears in the mirror above the check-out area.

Hint 109: A Mickey hat with ears hides at one corner of each of two outside signs for the Mad Hatter shop.

- Castle Heraldry Shoppe

Hint 110: Near the Castle Heraldry Shoppe, a classic Mickey is in the bottom center of the painted scroll trim at the edges of a mailbox outside. Also look for the classic Mickeys wearing "Mickey's Sorcerer's Hat." They're repeated at the end of some of the branches in the scrollwork at the top and bottom of the mailbox.

Tomorrowland

- Redd Rockett's Pizza Port

Hint 111: On a wall inside the restaurant, groupings of circles are on a poster entitled "Adventure Thru Inner Space." The circles in the middle right of the poster approximate a classic Mickey.

- The Star Trader shop

Hint 112: Classic Mickey holes are in some upright merchandise display poles.

Frontierland

- entrance walkway

Hint 113: A cannon sits to the right, just past the Frontierland sign on the entrance walkway from the central hub. In the tongue behind the cannon is a classic Mickey, formed by a hole and two bolts.

- River Belle Terrace restaurant

Hint 114: The back of a child's highchair has a classic Mickey cutout.

Main Street, U.S.A.

Hint 115: To the right of the main entrance (as you enter), a painting hanging on the wall has three white roses that form an upside-down classic Mickey.

- Silhouette Studio

Hint 116: In the Silhouette Studio's front display window, the outer frame design of some of the displays have classic Mickey symbols. (These frames come and go, but a frame with classic Mickeys is usually on display.)

- Gibson Girl Ice Cream Parlor

Hint 117: A bejeweled lamp is hanging from the ceiling at the rear of the Gibson Girl Ice Cream Parlor. Along the lower part of the lamp, jewels are positioned to form classic Mickeys.

- Blue Ribbon Bakery

Hint 118: In a painting on the rear wall behind the middle of the counter, look near a cow for a sack filled with fruit and vegetables. The large yellow fruit at the top of the sack forms a sideways classic Mickey with two limes.

- fruit cart

Hint 119: A green classic Mickey hides on an axle under a fruit cart that is usually positioned midway along Main Street near the Disney Clothiers shop.

- Market House

Hint 120: In the rear of the Market House, a side door leads to a Cast Member door. A light cover with classic Mickeys is on the wall just past the side door.

- Main Street Cinema

Hint 121: Inside Main Street Cinema, some of the recessed lights at the sides of the steps are shaped like classic Mickeys.

Hint 122: Outside, near Main Street Cinema, a "Casting Agency" sign on a door has two classic Mickeys in the design, one at the top and one at the bottom.

- Penny Arcade

Hint 123: Inside the Penny Arcade, in the rear section, a small classic Mickey rests between the play buttons on a game machine called "Pinocchio, Make Him Dance."

Frontierland

- Fantasmic!

Hint 124: During the show, a classic Mickey appears on the water screen, outlined by white foam. You can spot it just before the scene with Mickey and the whirlpool.

Fireworks show

Hint 125: Disneyland's fireworks show usually features a cluster of three exploding shells that form a classic Mickey.

Main Entrance Plaza between the Theme Parks

Hint 126: Some of the engraved personalized brick plaques at your feet feature a bell design. The bell ringer is a classic Mickey. (You'll also find decorative Mickey images on these plaques.)

Hint 127: The bottoms of some of the directional sign-poles in the plaza have classic Mickey indentations.

Disney's California Adventure Scavenger Hunt

● ●

★ Arrive at the entrance turnstiles (with your admission ticket) 30 minutes before the official opening time.

★ After entering the park, bear right to the Golden State area and ride **Soarin' Over California**.

Clue 1: Pay attention to the pre-show video for Mickey ears.
2 points

Clue 2: In the pre-show video, find some clothing characters.
4 points for spotting two Hidden Characters

Clue 3: On the ride, look left for a Mickey balloon.
4 points

Clue 4: Then quickly look right for a Mickey shadow on the golf course.
4 points

Clue 5: Watch the ball hurtling toward you.
5 points

Clue 6: Search the sky over the castle for a Hidden Mickey.
3 points

★ Walk back across Sunshine Plaza to Hollywood Pictures Backlot. Ride **The Twilight Zone Tower of Terror™**.

Clues 7 and 8: Spot a Mickey doll during the pre-show and on the ride.
3 points for each sighting; 6 points total

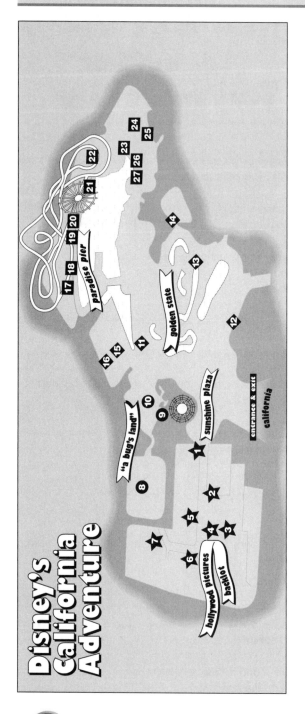

sunshine plaza

★ hollywood pictures backlot

1 "Playhouse Disney—Live on Stage!"
2 MuppetVision 3D
3 Monsters, Inc. Mike & Sulley to the Rescue!
4 The Hollywood Backlot Stage
5 Disney Animation:
   Turtle Talk with Crush
   Animation Academy
   Character Close-Up
   Sorcerer's Workshop
6 "Disney's Aladdin—A Musical Spectacular"
7 The Twilight Zone Tower of Terror™

● "a bug's land"

8 Flik's Fun Fair:
   Tuck and Roll's Drive 'Em Buggies
   Francis' Ladybug Boogie
   Flik's Flyers
   Princess Dot Puddle Park
   Heimlich's Chew Chew Train
9 It's Tough to be a Bug!
10 Bountiful Valley Farm

◆ golden state

11 Walt Disney Imagineering Blue Sky Cellar
12 Soarin' Over California
13 Grizzly River Run
14 Redwood Creek Challenge Trail

15 The Bakery Tour
16 Mission Tortilla Factory

■ paradise pier

17 California Screamin'
18 King Triton's Carousel
19 Toy Story Mania!
20 Games of the Boardwalk
21 Mickey's Fun Wheel
22 Maliboomer
23 Orange Stinger
24 S.S. rustworthy
25 Mulholland Madness
26 Jumpin' Jellyfish
27 Golden Zephyr

63

Clue 9: Find Mickey along the exit after the ride.
3 points

★ Go to **Monsters, Inc. Mike & Sulley to the Rescue!** and line up.

Clue 10: Study the inside queue walls for a Hidden Mickey.
3 points

Clue 11: Watch the pre-show video monitor in the queue for a Hidden Mickey.
3 points

Clue 12: Before you board your vehicle, spot those headlights again!
2 points

Clue 13: At the beginning of the ride, search the sky-line for a tiny Hidden Mickey.
5 points

Clue 14: Don't miss the moving Mickey shadow on a wall along the ride!
5 points

Clue 15: On the ride, look for a Hidden Mickey on a character.
4 points

Clue 16: Stay alert for Mickey near a monitor screen.
3 points

★ Cross Sunshine Plaza and walk by "a bug's land" to Paradise Pier. Turn left and pass by Ariel's Grotto restaurant and line up for **Toy Story Mania!**

Clue 17: Spot a classic Mickey at the loading dock.
2 points

Clue 18: While on the ride, find Mickey's ears on the wall.
4 points

Clue 19: After you exit, search for Mickey along the promenade.
4 points

★ Walk to **California Screamin'** and ride if you're brave enough!

Clue 20: Stay alert while you're screaming for a classic Mickey below you on the ground.
4 points

Clue 21: Find Mickey on a sign along the exit.
2 points

★ Stroll to **Mulholland Madness** in Paradise Pier.

Clue 22: Study the outside billboards at *Mulholland Madness* for a Hidden Mickey on a car.
4 points

Clue 23: Find another Hidden Mickey on a billboard by a house.
3 points

Clue 24: Spot two Hidden Mickeys around the beginning of the entrance queue.
4 points for finding both

Clue 25: Locate Mickey on a wall at the loading dock.
4 points

Clue 26: Don't miss Mickey near the floor of the loading dock!
5 points

★ Check out **Jumpin' Jellyfish**.

Clue 27: Study the outside of the attraction for a classic Mickey.
4 points

★ Stroll over to **Maliboomer**.

Clue 28: Study the attraction for a Hidden Mickey.
3 points

★ Enter the **Sideshow Shirts store**, not far from *Mickey's Fun Wheel*.

Clue 29: Look around for a small Hidden Mickey near some nails.
4 points

Clue 30: Search for a Hidden Mickey on a wall inside the store.
4 points

★ Search inside the **Man Hat 'n' Beach store**.

Clue 31: Locate a Hidden Mickey on a merchandise stand.
3 points

★ Enter the **Point Mugu Tattoo store**.

Clue 32: Spot a Hidden Mickey on a wall.
3 points

★ Now stroll along the **promenade**.

Clue 33: Search the *Games of the Boardwalk* buildings for a Hidden Mickey.
3 points

Clue 34: Find Donald Duck on the promenade outside *King Triton's Carousel*.
3 points

★ Stroll around Paradise Bay to the **Treasures in Paradise shop**.

Clue 35: Find a Hidden Mickey on an animal inside the store.
2 points total for one or more

Clue 36: Look for Mickey in a painting.
4 points

★ Walk to "a bug's land." Enjoy **Heimlich's Chew Chew Train**.

Clue 37: Watch for Mickey in the rocks.
4 points

Clue 38: Look for Mickey on a **snack stand** in "a bug's land."
3 points

★ Consider lunch at the restaurant of your choice, or try one of the nearby counter-service eateries: Pacific Wharf Cafe (salads, chowders, etc.) or Cocina Cucamonga Mexican Grill.

★ While at lunch, check your Times Guide for the next show in Hyperion Theater (the show there as we go to press is *"Disney's Aladdin—A Musical Spectacular"*).

★ At the time you've chosen, walk to the far side of Hollywood Pictures Backlot to see the stage show at **Hyperion Theater**.

Clue 39: Look around for a Hidden Mickey inside the theater, near the seats.
3 points

★ Walk to **The Bakery Tour** in Golden State.

Clue 40: Locate Mickey inside the entrance to the tour.
2 points

★ Check out the **Blue Sky Cellar** for some Hidden Mickeys.

Clue 41: Study the sign outside.
4 points

Clue 42: Now admire Mickey in the first mural inside.
4 points

Clue 43: Find a classic Mickey in the main room.
3 points

★ Mosey straight ahead to the **Redwood Creek Challenge Trail**.

Clues 44 to 46: Tarry at the large trail map just inside the entrance to spot three classic Mickeys.
5 points for finding all three

Clue 47: Mickey is near a cave inside the trail area.
3 points

★ Check out the **Rushin' River Outfitters shop** near *Grizzly River Run*.

Clue 48: Search for Hidden Mickeys on the merchandise inside the shop.
3 points

Clue 49: Look for Mickey on Mater **across from Soarin' Over California**.
4 points

★ Amble over to the **Taste Pilots' Grill**.

Clue 50: Study the walls inside for two Hidden Mickeys.
2 points each; 4 points total

★ Cross Sunshine Plaza to Hollywood Pictures Backlot. Stop by **MuppetVision 3D**.

Clue 51: Watch for a Hidden Mickey in the pre-show.
3 points

Clue 52: Near the end of the main show, find classic Mickeys on hats.
4 points

Clue 53: Try to spot Mickey balloons during the show.
3 points

★ Stand outside the **Disney Animation Building** and look up.

Clue 54: Find a Hidden Mickey.
3 points

Clue 55: Spot Hidden Mickeys along the Disney Animation building's entrance hall.
3 points total for one or more

Clue 56: Find a Hidden Mickey at the entrance area to *Turtle Talk with Crush*. (Enjoy the show if the timing is right.)
2 points

Clue 57: Search for a classic Hidden Mickey inside the *Animation Academy*.
3 points

Clue 58: Walk through the *Sorcerer's Workshop* and locate two Hidden Mickeys on the wall.
4 points total for spotting both

Clue 59: Find two Hidden Mickeys in the wall posters outside.
4 points total for spotting both

Clue 60: Study the pictures in the glass nearby for a classic Mickey.
3 points

Clue 61: Search a display window nearby for a Hidden Mickey.
3 points

Clue 62: Now look for Mickey on the ceiling inside the shop.
4 points

★ Cross the street to **Schmoozies**.

Clues 63 and 64: Check out the outside walls for Hidden Mickeys
5 points for finding two

★ Walk into the **Studio Store** near the entrance to *MuppetVision 3D*.

Clue 65: Find a Hidden Mickey.
4 points

★ Head for **Sunshine Plaza** to search for more Hidden Mickeys.

Clue 66: Study the pavement in front of the Sun Fountain for a Hidden Mickey.
5 points

Clue 67: Search for another Hidden Mickey under a cement bench.
5 points

Clue 68: Find some Hidden Mickeys near trees.
2 points

★ Enter the **Greetings from California store**.

Clue 69: Spot Mickey on a reel of film.
2 points

Clue 70: In the next room, spot Mickey on a car.
4 points

Clue 71: Find a camera Hidden Mickey in the following room.
3 points

Clues 72 and 73: Move on into the next room and look around for two underwater Mickeys.
4 points total for spotting both

Clue 74 : In this same room, glance up for Mickey.
3 points

Clue 75: In the next room, locate two Mickeys on the beach.
4 points total for spotting both

Clue 76: **Outside the Greetings from California store**, search high for a Hidden Mickey.
4 points

Clue 77: Walk over to the **Engine Ears Toys store** and find two classic Mickeys on the walls.
5 points total for spotting both

Clue 78: Spot a Hidden Mickey on the wall inside **Baker's Field Bakery**.
2 points

★ Exit Disney's California Adventure Park to the *main entrance plaza between the theme parks*.

Clue 79: Study the pavement just outside the exit gates for a Hidden Mickey.
5 points

Clue 80: Spot larger Hidden Mickeys farther out in the entrance plaza.
2 points for one or more

Clue 81: Look over some trees in the plaza for Hidden Mickeys.
3 points for one or more

Clue 82: Check out ticket buildings for classic Mickeys.
2 points for one or more

Total Points for Disney's California Adventure Park =

How'd You Do?

Up to 108 points – Bronze
109 to 215 points – Silver
216 points and over – Gold
270 points – Perfect Score

**Caution:
Don't peek at this
section unless you
really want help!**

Golden State

- Soarin' Over California

Hint 1: In the pre-show video to *Soarin'*, a man is asked to remove his Mickey Mouse ears.

Hint 2: In the *Soarin'* pre-show, a boy sitting in his ride seat is wearing a shirt with a Grumpy logo and shorts sporting Mickey Mouse.

Hint 3: When you soar over the hills and spot a golf course, look immediately to your lower left and find a golf cart. The man standing on the other side of the cart is holding a blue Mickey balloon.

Hint 4: Look to the right side of the golf course. About halfway along the fairway is a slightly distorted classic Mickey shadow on the green grass formed by a cluster of three trees. The "ears" of the shadow Mickey touch the right side of the white cart path.

Hint 5: Look straight ahead and down to the golf course. Spot the man about to swing a golf club. When he strikes the golf ball, it will head directly toward you. Watch the ball's rotation to see the dark classic Mickey on the surface of the ball.

Hint 6: You complete your *Soarin'* ride over Disneyland. Watch the evening fireworks explode before you; the second burst forms a huge classic Mickey in the sky.

Hollywood Pictures Backlot

- *The Twilight Zone Tower of Terror*™

Hint 7: In the pre-show video in the library, the little girl is holding a Mickey doll.

Hint 8: On the ride, the little girl appears again, still holding the Mickey doll in her left hand.

Hint 9: Circles on the front of some of the cameras in displays along the exit form classic Mickeys. You'll find one of the best images on a camera behind and to the right side of the photo purchase counter. Look for it on the right side of the second shelf.

- *Monsters, Inc. Mike & Sulley to the Rescue!*

Hint 10: On the "Monstropolis Cab Co." wall poster, the taxicab headlights form an upside-down classic Mickey.

Hint 11: During the video loop on the queue monitors, a taxi appears with the words "Please Proceed" on the front bumper. The headlights of this vehicle are shaped like upside-down classic Mickeys.

Hint 12: The taxi in the pre-show video with the upside-down headlight classic Mickeys is pictured on the side of your vehicle.

Hint 13: As your vehicle begins to move, look at the skyline behind a tall wall to your left. A tiny black classic Mickey is visible through holes along the top of the wall. Look along the skyline. You'll find this Mickey below the green "Downtown" sign and to the left of a tall vertical pipe behind the wall.

Hint 14: To the left of your ride vehicle, a side-profile shadow of Mickey moves from left to right along the windows in the wall of the Harryhausen's scene.

Hint 15: Sulley appears several times during the ride. A dark classic Mickey marking is on Sulley's left upper thigh the last time he appears (by the pink door).

Hint 16: Near the end of the ride, a classic Mickey is formed by dials and gauges on a control panel under the right monitor screen.

Paradise Pier

- Toy Story Mania!

Hint 17: A classic Mickey is formed by three picture frames with *Toy Story* characters on the wall at the loading area.

Hint 18: During the ride, look for a drawing of a Ferris wheel on the wall. The tops of the Ferris wheel seats resemble Mickey's ears.

Hint 19: Across from *Toy Story Mania!*, Steamboat Willie Mickey is pictured on faux newspapers stacked at a drink stand.

- California Screamin'

Hint 20: When you're upside down in the loop, look at the ground to your left for a classic Mickey cement footing at the base of one of the vertical support poles. You can also spot this Mickey if you look right as you ride through the little hills that are over *Toy Story Mania!*

Hint 21: Classic Mickeys are atop the frames of the sample photos on the sign advertising the California Scream Cam. (You can see this Hidden Mickey without riding the coaster.)

- Mulholland Madness

Hint 22: Outside the ride, look for a blue license plate on a billboard under the "Mulholland Madness" sign. The license plate has a tiny classic Mickey in its upper right corner.

Hint 23: Outside the ride, find the billboard with Sunset Boulevard. One of the pools on the billboard is shaped like a classic Mickey.

Hint 24: On a wall mural to the left at the beginning of the entrance queue, a child in a car is holding a red Mickey balloon. A dark classic Mickey is on the mural above the balloon.

Hint 25: A tiny black classic Mickey is at the upper right of a "Cast Only" license plate on the wall near the vehicle loading area.

Hint 26: A silver classic Mickey hides on a metal strip below the yellow fence and just above the floor to the right of the vehicles in the loading area.

- Jumpin' Jellyfish

Hint 27: Bubbles on a support pole on the right (as you face the attraction) form a sideways classic Mickey. You can see it best from the play area to the right of the attraction.

- Maliboomer

Hint 28: Classic Mickey holes are in the bottom yellow supports for the rider seats.

- Sideshow Shirts store

Hint 29: Toward the front of the store, find a painting of a man lying on a bed of nails. A small classic Mickey marking is in the wood on the side of the bed.

Hint 30: A painting of a woman named Betty is on the rear wall of the store. A classic Mickey is etched in the wood on the middle of the right side of the picture frame.

- Man Hat 'n' Beach store

Hint 31: On a merchandise stand inside the store, a classic Mickey is on the back of an octopus's head.

- Point Mugu Tattoo store

Hint 32: On the rear wall near the ceiling, a classic Mickey is on a sign between the words "Paradise" and "Pier."

- Along the promenade

Hint 33: White classic Mickey designs are under the high eaves of the *Games of the Boardwalk* building with the "Paradise Pier Amusements Co." sign.

Hint 34: A row of Donald Ducks is atop each of two large gazebos next to the lake near *King Triton's Carousel*.

- Treasures in Paradise shop

Hint 35: A classic Mickey adorns the lower sides of some carousel lions' saddles in store displays.

Hint 36: In the "Azalea" painting of a lady behind a service counter, a classic Mickey is formed by circles in the area where the wide belt loops connect below her waist.

"a bug's land"

- Heimlich's Chew Chew Train

Hint 37: Near the end of the ride, the train stops prior to re-entering the station. Three rocks in the shape of a classic Mickey are embedded in a hill to the right of the ride vehicle. If you are seated in row 4, the Hidden Mickey will be close by.

Hint 38: A classic Mickey made of cherries is on the front of a fruit drink stand, which is often located near *Heimlich's Chew Chew Train*.

Hollywood Pictures Backlot

- show at Hyperion Theater

Hint 39: Classic Mickeys are at the top center of the frames over several of the doors inside the theater.

Golden State

- The Bakery Tour

Hint 40: On a table in a corner of the first room, you'll see bread rolls. Sometimes they're shaped like Mickey and other times they are imprinted with him.

- Blue Sky Cellar

Hint 41: On an outdoor sign for Walt Disney Imagineering Blue Sky Cellar, a tiny classic Mickey hides at the lower left in the swirling path of sparkles.

Hint 42: A cloud image of Sorcerer Mickey is at the lower left of the blue mural just inside the entrance.

Hint 43: A black classic Mickey lies on a paint palette in an Imagineering art display in the main room.

- Redwood Creek Challenge Trail

Hint 44: On the top left side of the trail map, a group of three rocks in a stream forms a classic Hidden Mickey.

Hint 45: Three circles at the middle left side of the trail map form a classic Mickey in foam. He's just to the left of the mouth of the water slide.

Hint 46: On the lower left side of the trail map, three log seats in the Ahwahnee Camp Circle are arranged to make a classic Mickey.

Hint 47: At the rear of the trail area, three gray rocks embedded in the ground in front of Kenai's Spirit Cave form a classic Mickey.

- Rushin' River Outfitters shop

Hint 48: On some of the stuffed grizzly bears, the rear pads on the bottoms of the paws are shaped like classic Mickeys.

- near Soarin' Over California

Hint 49: In Mater's Character Greeting area, a classic Mickey wing nut sits on top of the air cleaner on his engine.

- Taste Pilots' Grill

Hint 50: A photo of an engine shows a classic Mickey shape. The photo is in two places: to the left of the food order area over an exit door and also to the right of the food order area on the right rear wall.

Hollywood Pictures Backlot

- MuppetVision 3D

Hint 51: Early in the pre-show on the monitors, check the screen for a test pattern with a classic Mickey shape.

Hint 52: Near the end of the main show, during the Muppets' celebration with marching bands and fireworks, some of the band members wear blue Colonial-style hats with red tabs on the side. The tabs have classic Mickeys in the center.

Hint 53: Near the end of the movie, after the cannon shoots holes in the theater, some of the observers outside are holding Mickey balloons.

- Disney Animation Building

Hint 54: A small classic Mickey sits atop the flagpole over the front of the Animation building.

Hint 55: In the mosaic lettering on the building's entrance (and exit) walls, large and small circles form many classic Mickeys.

Hint 56: Some classic Mickey circles are in the carpet right in front of the entrance doors to the *Turtle Talk with Crush* theater.

Hint 57: A drum set shaped like a classic Mickey sits on a shelf high above the stage inside the *Animation Academy*. You'll also find many decorative Mickey images on and around the stage.

Hint 58: In the *Sorcerer's Workshop* area, Sorcerer Mickey is on the left wall toward the end of the room. He's encircled by classic Mickey bubbles. Nearby on the left wall, a classic Mickey is intertwined in the middle of a treble clef.

Hint 59: Shadows of boys with Mickey ears decorate the bottoms of two posters on the wall outside; one poster is entitled "Turtle Talk" and the other "Toy Story Zoetrope."

Hint 60: In the tall green glass wall outside, an upside-down classic Mickey made of dots floats above and to the left of the rightmost fairy's pointed hat. The Hidden Mickey is about halfway up the right side of the glass wall.

Hint 61: In an outside display window of the Off the Page shop, the last of several Dalmatians has an upside-down classic Mickey made of spots on its rear thigh.

Hint 62: Bubbles form a classic Mickey in front of the upper leg of an alligator on a drawing hanging from the ceiling in the middle of the store.

- Schmoozies

Hint 63: Face Schmoozies from the street, and then walk to the left side of the shop. There are two murals on the left wall. The one on the right contains classic Mickeys formed by round green and white pieces of glass.

Hint 64: Face the shop from Hollywood Boulevard. A classic Mickey formed by three tan stones hides to the right of a knife tip and above a pink cup on the right side of the rightmost mural on the front of the shop.

- Studio Store

Hint 65: A classic Mickey formed of photo frames hides on an inside wall of the store to the upper left of a window facing the main boulevard.

Sunshine Plaza

Hint 66: As you stand facing the Sun Fountain, look at the straight "rays" in the cement with glass pieces embedded in them. Find the second ray from the right side. A small, light brown classic Mickey lies in the cement about 10 to 12 feet from the fountain and several inches to the left of this second ray.

Hint 67: Face away from the Sun Fountain and locate a cement bench to your right that surrounds a planted area. A small classic Mickey is etched in the ground under the right side of the round lip that juts out from the bench.

Hint 68: Grates around the base of trees in Sunshine Plaza and elsewhere have classic Mickey circles.

- Greetings from California store

Hint 69: In the room next to the candy store, a classic Mickey is in the middle of a large film reel that hangs from the ceiling above a check-out area.

Hint 70: In the "K-GOOF" mural on a wall, a black classic Mickey is on the rear bumper of Goofy's car.

Hint 71: In one of the store's middle rooms, a huge camera on a wall has a small, black classic Mickey on its flashbulb.

Hint 72: Go to the store's photo preview and pickup area. To the left of the counters, a classic Mickey floats in a bubble above Goofy's head on the Goofy mural on the left wall.

Hint 73: On a mural on the opposite side of the room, a black classic Mickey is snorkeling on Mickey's swim trunks.

Hint 74: Stand at the photo pickup desk with the Goofy mural to your left. A purple classic Mickey is on the ceiling above you amid the recessed lights.

Hint 75: Classic Mickeys are in the sand at the lower right of two beach murals on opposite sides of the next room.

Hint 76: Outside the store, to the left of the first "Greetings from California" sign, look for a sign that says "Premiere" and pictures a stylized theater with searchlights and a ticket booth. A small white classic Mickey is the ticket seller in the booth. He's in the middle window, under the word "Premiere."

- Engine Ears Toys store

Hint 77: In the middle of the store and to the left, a classic Mickey shadow hides under a large orange on a framed "Paradise Pier" poster. Nearby on a round "Golden State" poster, a tiny classic Mickey made of water droplets can be found at the upper right of a grapefruit half.

- Baker's Field Bakery

Hint 78: In a display on the wall to the right, a plate and two dishes form a classic Mickey.

Main Entrance Plaza between the Theme Parks

Hint 79: This classic Mickey is embedded in the pavement between the big "R" (in "CALIFORNIA") and the exit turnstiles from the park. It's about 14 feet behind the slanted leg of the "R" and near reddish cement.

Hint 80: Four l+arge classic Mickeys are arranged around a compass-like design in the pavement of the entrance plaza.

Hint 81: Green ironwork gratings surround some tree trunks in the entrance plaza. Tiny classic Mickey fasteners hold the ironwork bands in place.

Hint 82: In the general entrance plaza, classic Mickey holes are inside the braces that hold up ticket booth counters.

Notes

Downtown Disney District & Resort Hotel Scavenger Hunt

• •

Because you may want to hunt only one area at a time, I've listed the perfect score for each area in parentheses after its name in the Clues section.

Downtown Disney District
(30 points)

Begin your Downtown Disney search at about 11:00 a.m. to give yourself time to complete this hunt.

★ Check out the **Disney Vault 28** shop.

Clue 1: Locate a classic Mickey in a window of the store.
3 points

Clue 2: Search for two Mickeys on a wall.
5 points for spotting both

★ Your next stop is **Marceline's Confectionery** store.

Clue 3: Find a Hidden Mickey outside the store.
3 points

★ Continue on to **Naples Ristorante e Pizzeria**.

Clue 4: Look up for a Hidden Mickey.
3 points

★ Walk to **Quiksilver Boardriders Club Store**.

Clue 5: Search for a Hidden Mickey outside the store.
4 points

★ Stroll over to the **World of Disney** store nearby.

85

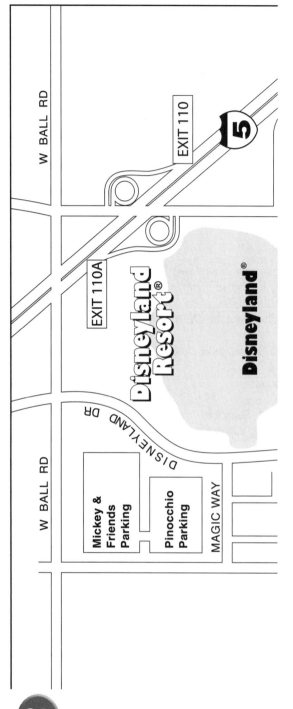

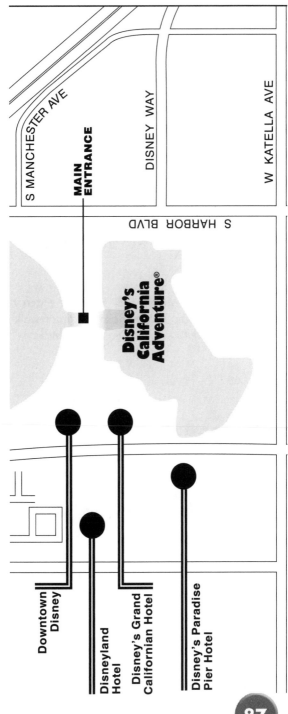

S MANCHESTER AVE

DISNEY WAY

W KATELLA AVE

MAIN ENTRANCE

S HARBOR BLVD

Disney's California Adventure®

Downtown Disney

Disneyland Hotel

Disney's Grand Californian Hotel

Disney's Paradise Pier Hotel

Clue 6: Find Hidden Mickeys outside World of Disney.
1 point total for one or more

Clue 7: Locate a classic Mickey near the ceiling in the Princess room in the middle of the store.
4 points

Clue 8: Keep looking for Mickey on another mural in the Princess room.
5 points for finding all seven

★ Exit the World of Disney, and walk toward the **main entrance plaza** between the parks.

Clue 9: Study some kiosks near the entrance plaza for Hidden Mickeys.
2 points

★ Now go to the **Mickey & Friends Parking Structure** tram stop nearby. Take a tram or walk to the Parking Structure to find some Hidden Mickeys.

Mickey & Friends Parking Structure
(21 points)

Clue 10: Stop and look up at the directional sign on the walkway near the tram stop.
2 points

Clue 11: Inside the parking structure, walk up to Level 2 (Daisy Level) and find a Hidden Mickey between poles 3A and 3B.
5 points

Clue 12: Also on Level 2, search for a Hidden Mickey near pole 2A.
4 points

Clue 13: Look around for Mickey on a sign.
3 points

Clue 14: The address for Disneyland and Mickey & Friends Parking Structure is 1313 S. Harbor Blvd. Since "M" is the thirteenth letter, two

13's correspond to two "M's", Mickey Mouse's initials.
5 points if you can find the address posted

Clue 15: On the tram to the parks, spot Mickey on a pole.
2 points

★ Make your way back to Downtown Disney, then walk to **Disney's Grand Californian Hotel & Spa**.

Disney's Grand Californian Hotel & Spa
(50 points)

- outside the main entrance

Clue 16: Outside the main entrance, look for a side-profile Hidden Mickey on a panel.
5 points

Clue 17: In this same area, find a classic Mickey on a panel.
3 points

- lobby area and nearby hallway

Clue 18: Enter the lobby and search low for a Hidden Mickey.
3 points

Clue 19: Study the front of the registration counters for a "conductor Mickey."
5 points

Clue 20: Look on the front of the registration counters for a classic Mickey.
4 points

Clue 21: Search the front of the registration counters for a Hidden Tinker Bell.
5 points

Clue 22: Glance behind the registration counters for a classic Mickey.
4 points

Clue 23: Find a Hidden Mickey facing the hotel's main lobby.
5 points

Clue 24: Spot a Mickey image on a desk.
3 points

Clue 25: Look for Mickey in the hallway not far from the registration counters. (It's to your left when you come in through the main entrance.)
4 points

Clue 26: Search for Mickey near the fireplace.
3 points

Clue 27: Find four Mickey images on a ship.
4 points total for spotting all four

- Hearthstone Lounge

Clue 28: Check around the Hearthstone Lounge for a Hidden Mickey.
2 points

★ If you're hungry, snack inside Hearthstone Lounge or try to get seated for lunch at Storytellers Cafe.

★ Stroll over to **Disney's Paradise Pier Hotel**.

Disney's Paradise Pier Hotel
(40 points)

- outside the front entrance

Clue 29: Spot Mickey on a wall outside the front entrance of the hotel.
4 points

- inside the hotel

Clue 30: Spot Mickey in the main hotel lobby.
4 points

Clue 31: Look for a wall painting inside the hotel with a Hidden Mickey.
3 points

Clue 32: Find a Hidden Mickey near the elevators.
3 points

Clue 33: Mickey is near the swimming pool.
2 points

Clue 34: Don't miss Mickey in the Game Room!
2 points

Clue 35: Locate Mickey in a photo in a hallway near the lobby.
5 points

★ Search for classic Mickeys in the hotel's **PCH Grill** restaurant.

- in the PCH Grill

Clue 36: Study the carpet.
2 points

Clue 37: Search for Mickeys of different sizes in the wall décor.
3 points total for spotting both

Clue 38: Look for Mickey on lamps.
2 points

Clue 39: Find Mickey in a picture.
1 point

Clue 40: Scan the ceiling.
2 points

Clue 41: Search for classic Mickeys camouflaged on two different surfboards.
4 points total for spotting both

Clue 42: Find two Mickeys on entrance doors.
2 points total for spotting both

- rear entrance to the hotel

Clue 43: You can't miss Mickey outside the first floor rear entrance.
1 point

★ Your final stop is the ***Disneyland Hotel***.

Disneyland Hotel
(41 points)

- *lobby and entrance areas*

Clue 44: Inside the hotel lobby in the Magic Tower, look down for some Hidden Mickeys.
2 points for each of three Hidden Mickeys; 6 points total

Clue 45: Study the lobby walls for Hidden Mickeys.
4 points

Clue 46: Step outside the front entrance to spot Hidden Mickeys in the nearby parking lot.
1 point

Clue 47: Take the central lobby elevator down a floor to find two Hidden Mickeys, one complete and one partial.
4 points total for finding both

Clue 48: Peer inside a gift shop for some Hidden Mickeys.
3 points total for one or more

Clue 49: Look for two Mickey images in the Guest Services office near the main lobby.
4 points total for spotting both.

Clue 50: Locate Mickey in the telephone area.
1 point

- *around the hotel complex*

Clue 51: Spot two Hidden Mickeys in the Convention Center area.
2 points total for finding both

Clue 52: Peer inside Goofy's Theater to spot some Hidden Mickeys.
3 points total for finding three different sizes

Clue 53: Stroll the hallways in the Sleeping Beauty Pavilion for Hidden Mickeys.
2 points

Clue 54: Look around for two more Mickey images near the Sleeping Beauty Pavilion.
4 points for spotting both

Clue 55: Walk inside Hook's Pointe restaurant and find a Hidden Mickey. (You may need to return later if it's not yet open.)
3 points

Clue 56: Explore the lobby areas of the Dreams Tower and the Wonder Tower for two more Hidden Mickeys.
4 points total for spotting both

Total Points for Downtown Disney and the Resort Hotels =

How'd You Do?

A perfect score for this scavenger hunt is 182. But here is a breakdown by area, so that you can compare your score with the perfect score for the areas you've covered. You'll find the perfect score for each section in parentheses. Give yourself gold if you score at least 80% of the total available points. (That would be 146 if you covered all five areas.)

Downtown Disney (30)
Mickey & Friends Parking Structure (21)
Disney's Grand Californian Hotel & Spa (50)
Disney's Paradise Pier Hotel (40)
Disneyland Hotel (41)

**Caution:
Don't peek at this
section unless you
really want help!**

- Disney Vault 28

Hint 1: A classic Mickey head is above crossbones in the window just below the right side of the large "Disney Vault 28" outside sign.

Hint 2: A tiny classic Mickey is stuck on the upper right of the large metal vault door that forms the back wall of the entrance vestibule of the store, while an upside-down classic Mickey can be found on the vault door's lower right.

- Marceline's Confectionery

Hint 3: On the sign in front of the store, swirls in the letters "M" and "C" combine to form a classic Mickey.

- Naples Ristorante e Pizzeria

Hint 4: In front of the restaurant, near the top edge of the pizza sign at the 1:00 posi-

95

tion, three circular pepperonis form a sideways classic Mickey.

- Quiksilver Boardriders Club Store

Hint 5: Outside in front of the store, a classic Mickey in the cement walkway is directly below a vertical red surfboard on the wall.

- World of Disney

Hint 6: Blue classic Mickeys are on the corners of the large sign over the entrance doorway to the store.

Hint 7: In a mural near the ceiling on the left side of the Princess room, a white classic Mickey is on an archway to the right of several Dalmatians.

Hint 8: Seven small red classic Mickeys are on a mural of the world behind the service counter in the Princess room.

- entrance plaza

Hint 9: Classic Mickey-shaped eave supports are on several kiosks in Downtown Disney near the main park entrance plaza.

Mickey & Friends Parking Structure

Hint 10: A classic Mickey sits atop the sign which points the way to Mickey & Friends Parking Structure.

Hint 11: A classic Mickey is etched in the cement between poles 3A and 3B, next to an unnumbered pole and under an "Emergency" sign.

Hint 12: A classic Mickey is etched in the cement two car stalls over from pole 2A, toward the exit drive path.

Hint 13: Inside on the parking structure walls, a black classic Mickey is atop the yellow "Caution U-Turn" signs.

Hint 14: Ask a Cast Member where you can

find "1313" as the posted address on Mickey & Friends Parking Structure.

Hint 15: Classic Mickeys are on top of the light poles that line the tram path from the Mickey & Friends Parking Structure to the parks.

Disney's Grand Californian Hotel & Spa

- outside the main entrance

Hint 16: A pillar just outside the main entrance is covered with colorful panels. On the rear panel, a side profile of Mickey's full face is between the outside branches of a tree, about three-quarters of the way up the tree.

Hint 17: On this same rear panel, a classic Mickey clearing is at the middle bottom of the tree branches.

- lobby area and nearby hallway

Hint 18: As you enter the lobby of Disney's Grand Californian, look for a rug with the hotel logo. A small classic Mickey is in the middle of the tree on the rug just above where the leaves and branches start.

Hint 19: A small side view of Mickey Mouse is sculpted in tile on the front desk. Toward the middle of the long counter, look for dancing bears on a panel in a depression in the desk. Mickey Mouse is conducting with a wand to the right of the white bear.

Hint 20: To the right of "conductor Mickey" is a brown, raised classic Mickey on the lower middle part of a tree.

Hint 21: To the left of "conductor Mickey" is a figure of Tinker Bell near and to the immediate left of a flat writing surface (check-in or check-out section).

Hint 22: On a fabric mural on the far left side of the rear wall behind the registration counters, is a dark classic Mickey in the lower middle part of the branches in the leftmost tree.

Hint 23: A classic Mickey depression is on the face of the Grandfather Clock in the main lobby.

Hint 24: A classic Mickey hole is in the middle front of a desk, high up under the projecting lip of the desktop. The desk is usually at the rear left of the main lobby.

Hint 25: In the nearby hallway, classic Mickeys are in the corners of the frame of a painting that hangs on the wall near the restrooms. The painting shows a rocky and mountainous coastline.

Hint 26: Viewed from the main lobby, a classic Mickey made of round stones and tilted to the right is in the lower front part of the rock wall on the left side of the lobby fireplace.

Hint 27: A small model of a Disney Cruise ship is at the right side of the main lobby (as you enter from the front) and near the registration counters. Three classic Mickeys are on the bow and the two smokestacks, respectively, and a fourth Mickey's face is painted on the bottom of the pool at the rear (aft) of the ship.

- Hearthstone Lounge

Hint 28: Classic Mickey holes repeat near the outer rim of some of the large light fixtures hanging from the ceiling in the Hearthstone Lounge.

Disney's Paradise Pier Hotel

- outside the front entrance

Hint 29: Classic Mickey impressions are in the gray recessed wall just to the left of the front entrance (as you face the hotel).

- inside the hotel

Hint 30: A classic Mickey is on the back of

a shirt at the lower right of a picture that's hanging on the wall. It's across from the main lobby entrance doors and near the elevators.

Hint 31: Rocks form a (slightly distorted) classic Mickey at the upper right of a painting on the stairwell wall between the first and second floors near the main elevators.

Hint 32: At the edges of the blue carpet in the hallways, large clams near starfish form classic Mickeys with smaller circles for "ears."

Hint 33: On the third floor, classic Mickeys adorn the top of the railing around the swimming pool.

Hint 34: Large partial classic Mickeys are at the top of palm trees along the wall of the Game Room near the lobby elevators.

Hint 35: On a wall across from the Pacific Ballroom, a red classic Mickey reflection is in a photo of a sunset over the water. You see the sun through pier supports.

- PCH Grill

Hint 36: A multicolored classic Mickey in swirls is part of the carpet design.

Hint 37: Small, black classic Mickeys hide on vertical wires on the wall, while a large, black partial classic Mickey hides higher up on the wall near the kitchen.

Hint 38: Black classic Mickeys are on the food lamps hanging in the kitchen area.

Hint 39: A large classic Mickey with the earth as Mickey's head is in a picture on the wall.

Hint 40: A large black classic Mickey is on a red kite on the ceiling.

Hint 41: On the restaurant's walls, two surfboards are decorated with classic Mickeys.

One contains Mickeys in fireworks. The other hides Mickeys in flowers.

Hint 42: A large, black, partial classic Mickey hides in one of the four glass panels on each of the double doors at the restaurant entrance.

- rear entrance

Hint 43: Classic Mickeys are atop short poles just outside the rear entrance to the hotel.

Disneyland Hotel

- lobby and entrance areas

Hint 44: In the lobby and registration area, a gold classic Mickey and two green classic Mickeys (of different sizes) are repeated in the carpet.

Hint 45: Full-face Mickeys (frontal view) are repeated in the light gold wallpaper in the central lobby.

Hint 46: Classic Mickeys are atop the light poles in the main entrance parking lot.

Hint 47: Below the Magic Tower's central lobby, look for the room where "Lost and Found" is located. A complete classic Mickey is formed by the silver push panels on a set of swinging doors, while a partial Mickey is on the push panel of the single door marked, "Cast Members Only."

Hint 48: Near the main lobby in the Magic Tower, Disney's Fantasia Shop and Donald's Gifts and Sundries both have side-profile Mickeys in their blue carpeting.

Hint 49: The backs of chairs in the Guest Services office form classic Mickeys and, on the desks, you'll find black classic Mickeys decorating the recessed panels under the marble desktops.

Hint 50: Classic Mickeys are atop dividers between phones in the phone bank area behind a wall with photos near the Convention Center.

- around the hotel complex

Hint 51: Inside the hotel, in the Convention Center area to the right, small classic Mickeys are repeated in the light blue sides of the carpet and giant gold classic Mickeys decorate the carpet's central area.

Hint 52: Classic Mickeys of various sizes and colors are in the carpet in Goofy's Theater, across from Steakhouse 55.

Hint 53: Near Goofy's Kitchen, classic Mickeys are in the red carpet in the hallways near both the Sleeping Beauty Pavilion and the Magic Kingdom Ballroom nearby.

Hint 54: On the bank of telephones near the hallway adjacent to the Sleeping Beauty Pavilion, classic Mickeys are on the light covers and Mickey silhouettes are on the dividers between the phones.

Hint 55: Near the check-in podium in Hook's Pointe restaurant, a classic Mickey is made from blue swirls on the floor. Walk past the podium to the right and turn around for the best view of the image.

Hint 56: As in the Magic Tower, Mickey's face is in the wallpaper and classic Mickeys are in the carpet in the Dreams and Wonder towers.

Notes

CHAPTER 5

Other Mickey Appearances

These Hidden Mickeys won't earn you any points, but you're bound to enjoy them if you're in the right place at the right time to see them.

Look for holiday Hidden Mickeys if you're at Disneyland during the Christmas season, or for that matter, any major holiday.

Other "Hidden" Mickeys – décor and deliberate – appear with some regularity throughout the Disneyland® Resort. Notice the Mickster on Disneyland brochures, maps and flags, Cast Member name tags, guest room keys, pay telephones and phone books, and restaurant and store receipts. The restaurants sometimes offer classic Mickey butter and margarine pats, pancakes and waffles, and pizzas and pasta, as well as Mickey napkins. They also arrange dishes and condiments to form classic Mickeys. Some condiment containers are even shaped like Mickey. Road signs on Disneyland property may sport Mickey ears, and Disneyland vehicles and monorails may display Mickey Mouse insignia.

Cleaning personnel will often spray the ground, windows, furniture, and other items with three circles of cleaning solution (a classic Mickey) before the final cleansing. Or they may leave three wet Mickey Mouse circles on the pavement after mopping! Mickey even decorates manhole covers, survey markers, and utility covers in the ground, as you've probably already discovered for yourself.

Enjoy all these Mickeys as you enjoy Disneyland. And if you want to take some home with you, rest assured that you can always find "Hidden" Mickeys on souvenir mugs, merchandise bags and boxes, T-shirts, and Christmas tree ornaments sold in the Disneyland shops. So even when you're far away from Disneyland, you can continue to spot Hidden Mickeys.

To see one from space, check out Google Earth and find the classic Mickey created by two palm-lined sidewalks on either side of Disneyland Drive approaching Katella Avenue—below and just to the right of Disney's Paradise Pier Hotel in the Google Earth image.

To access the image, go to GoogleEarth (download the program from GoogleEarth.com) and "Fly to" Disneyland, California by clicking on the magnifying glass next to the destination. Then scroll with your mouse to the left and down until you're just below the Paradise Pier hotel, and you'll see the palm-outlined Hidden Mickey. (The palm-lined sidewalks form the head and ears).

It's a distorted image, but the voters on my website liked it as a Hidden Mickey, and I think you will, too.

My Favorite Hidden Mickeys

• •

In this field guide, I've described more than 275 Hidden Mickeys at Disneyland. I enjoy every one of them, but the following are extra special to me. They're special because of their uniqueness, their deep camouflage (which makes them especially hard to find), or the "Eureka!" response they elicit when I spot them – or any combination of the above. Here then are my Favorite Hidden Mickeys at Disneyland. I apologize to you if your favorite Hidden Mickey is not (yet) on the list below.

My Top Ten

1. Conductor Mickey. Check the registration counter at Disney's Grand Californian Hotel & Spa and marvel at this magnificent (but tiny) rendition of Mickey conducting an imagined musical symphony for the dancing bears nearby.

2. Ship Mickey. Don't miss this faint, yellowish classic Mickey on the stern of a ship that sits high above the diners on a shelf near the ceiling in the Village Haus Restaurant in Disneyland's Fantasyland. Most folks in the dining room don't know he's there!

3. Mickey Smiling Out from a Tree. Out front of Disney's Grand Californian Hotel & Spa, observe a three-quarter view of Mickey's face peering out from between the branches of a tree on a ceramic panel on a column. Yes, he's smiling at you!

4. Tribute to Eeyore. Eeyore is watching you from above. He's in the rafters over the queue for *Indiana Jones Adventure*, in Disneyland's Adventureland. Give him a deserved salute!

5. Hidden Tink. All of us Tinker Bell fans can visit her at Disney's Grand Californian Hotel

& Spa; she's zipping around the registration desk. Catch her if you can!

6. Golf Ball Mickey. Keep your eyes peeled for this rotating classic Mickey on a golf ball, visible for only a second in *Soarin' Over California*, Golden State, Disney's California Adventure. Don't blink!

7. Mickey Goes Sailing. Pinocchio is a classic, and so is this hard to spot, elegant classic Mickey on a model ship case in *Pinocchio's Daring Journey*, Fantasyland, Disneyland.

8. Pavement Mickey #1. This first of three small and compelling classic Mickeys is in the pavement of the entrance plaza of Disney's California Adventure. Look behind the huge standing "R" (of "CALIFORNIA") near the entrance turnstiles. It sets the standard for the classic Mickey.

9. Pavement Mickey #2. The second pavement classic Mickey is in front of the Sunshine Plaza fountain in Disney's California Adventure. Let bystanders help you find it!

10. Pavement Mickey #3. Look at the ground under the lip of the cement bench near California Adventure's Sunshine Plaza fountain to find this classic. You may need to ask folks to move over to see it!

Ten Honorable Mentions

1. Clock Mickey. A subtle classic Mickey impression decorates the face of the grandfather clock in the lobby of Disney's Grand Californian Hotel & Spa. You'll be impressed!

2. Cryptic Symbol Mickey. You may need a flashlight for this one: the tiny classic Mickey symbol on the stone disk in the queue for *Indiana Jones Adventure*, Adventureland, Disneyland.

3. Garage Mickey. Make a special journey to find this classic Mickey in the cement of the Mickey & Friends Parking Structure. It's on Daisy Level, between poles 3A and 3B.

4. Foam Mickey. This classic Mickey hides in the foam on the *Fantasmic!* water screen, Frontierland, Disneyland. It's is a nice touch by the artists.

5. Skeleton Hat Mickey. Remember to look for Mickey ears in unusual places. How about on a skeleton's head in the *Indiana Jones Adventure* ride, Adventureland, Disneyland? I wonder if Mickey would approve?

6. Clock Tower Mickey. A side view of Mickey's face appears in a window of the Big Ben tower in *Peter Pan's Flight*, Fantasyland, Disneyland. Look back to spot Mickey in London!

7. Sunset Mickey. Journey to Disney's Paradise Pier Hotel to gawk at the sunset classic Mickey in the photo on the wall near the Pacific Ballroom. How did they do that?

8. Wood Knot Mickey. *Splash Mountain* is even more awesome if you stop to peer at the tiny classic Mickey impressed into the wood of the warning sign near the beginning of the outside entrance queue. Wow! Critter Country, Disneyland Park.

9. Frying Pan Mickey. In Disneyland's Adventureland, wait for the *Jungle Cruise* "Suwanee Lady" boat so you can appreciate this classic Mickey on a frying pan. One of a kind!

10. Rock Wall Mickey. Make a special effort to chase down the classic Mickey embossed on a rock wall that is near both the elevator for the *Disneyland Monorail* and *Finding Nemo Submarine Voyage* in Disneyland's Tomorrowland. You won't regret it!

Notes

CHAPTER 7

Don't Stop Now!

Hidden Mickey mania is contagious. The benign pastime of searching out Hidden Mickeys has escalated into a bona fide vacation mission for many Disneyland fans. I'm happy to add my name to the list of hunters. Searching for images of the Main Mouse can enhance a solo trip to the parks or a vacation for the entire family. Little ones delight in spotting and greeting Mickey Mouse characters in the parks and restaurants. As children grow, the Hidden Mickey game is a natural evolution of their fondness for the Mouse.

Join the search! With alert eyes and mind, you can spot Hidden Mickey classics and new ones waiting to be found. Even beginners have happened upon a new, unreported Hidden Mickey or two. As new attractions open and older ones get refurbished, new Hidden Mickeys await discovery.

The Disney entertainment phenomenon is unique in many ways, and Hidden Mickey mania is one manifestation of Disney's universal appeal. Join in the fun! Maybe I'll see you at Disneyland, marveling (like me) at the Hidden Gems. They're waiting patiently for you to discover them.

Index to Mickey's Hiding Places

Note: This Index includes only those rides, restaurants, shops, hotels and other places in the Disneyland Resort that harbor confirmed Hidden Mickeys. So if the attraction you're looking for isn't included, Mickey isn't hiding there. Or if he is, I haven't yet spotted him.

— Steve Barrett

The following abbreviations appear in this Index:

DL – Disneyland Park
CA – Disney's California Adventure Park
DD – Downtown Disney District
RH – Resort Hotel

www.intrepidtraveler.com